The Urban University

Today the urban university is the chief force in higher education. A relative newcomer to the American scene, it is educating hundreds of thousands of students while also answering basic community needs. With substantial responsibilities beyond those of providing an education for young people and adults of our cities, this type of university is charting the course of America's urban civilization.

The chancellor of the University of Wisconsin–Milwaukee identifies the unique character of this awakening educational giant and outlines the role the

(Continued on back flap)

The book makes clear the importance of urban education in the re-creation of our cities. It spells out with authority the special problems of city student and faculty, and outlines new courses that could provide the professional leadership urban America needs.

J. MARTIN KLOTSCHE received his doctorate from the University of Wisconsin–Madison, and taught history there and at Wisconsin State College in Milwaukee. Dr. Klotsche served as president of Wisconsin State College for ten years before becoming provost (1956) and then chancellor (1965) of the new University of Wisconsin–Milwaukee.

The Urban University:

AND THE FUTURE OF OUR CITIES

✦

J. MARTIN KLOTSCHE

Chancellor, University of Wisconsin–Milwaukee

HARPER & ROW, PUBLISHERS

NEW YORK

TO ROBERTA

FIRST EDITION

LIBRARY OF CONGRESS CATALOG CARD NUMBER: 66-10654

A-Q

✳ CONTENTS

$\rightarrowtail$ PREFACE

A BRIEF EXPLANATION OF THIS VOLUME IS IN ORDER. IT HAS
been written to highlight the place in American higher education
of the university located in the city. On the continent of Europe
cities and universities have long jostled each other and enjoyed
a symbiotic relationship. But this has not been as true in this
country. Yet a change is coming and the urban university that
accepts the challenge of its location can be instrumental in shaping
the future of our cities. Many individual histories of urban universities have been written, yet there is no single volume that treats
them as an entity. In a way this is strange, for urban universities
are growing more rapidly than others and will be expected in the
future to accommodate a disproportionate share of the exploding
college population.

This volume is not intended as a definitive treatment of the
urban university. Only a minimum amount of research on the
special and unique characteristics that distinguish it from other
colleges and universities has as yet been undertaken. It is hoped
that this volume which represents an effort to present within a
readable compass the main trends in what has been a neglected
area of American higher education will stimulate special studies in
depth on this subject.

My interest in this subject dates back to 1956 when the University of Wisconsin–Milwaukee was created to provide additional
educational opportunities for the people in heavily populated
southeastern Wisconsin. Subsequently, in the fall of 1960, the
University sponsored a conference on the role of the university in

an urban setting with representatives from 45 institutions located in major cities, 21 states, and 50 community organizations in attendance. The conference not only called attention to the common problems that universities located in cities are experiencing, but noted the increasingly important role that these institutions must play in the future growth of our cities. An extended visit to a number of urban universities in Great Britain and Europe in the fall of 1962 and many conversations and contacts with urban university people here at home further convinced me of the urgency of writing a volume on the growth and development of the urban university and the unlimited opportunities that lie before it at a time when our cities are becoming the central domestic concern of our people.

Many persons, far too numerous to mention, have contributed to making this volume possible. I owe special thanks to Fred Harvey Harrington, president of the University of Wisconsin. His vigorous and unqualified support of the University of Wisconsin–Milwaukee as a major campus of the system he heads, strongly backed by the Board of Regents, has resulted in laying the groundwork for a major urban university in the state's largest metropolitan center. Also, without his personal encouragement and enthusiastic support, this volume would not have been written.

An overriding acknowledgment must also be made to many nameless persons whose viewpoints have consciously or unconsciously contributed to my outlook. With the creation of the University of Wisconsin–Milwaukee ten years ago countless discussions and exchange of memoranda with faculty members and administrators, with municipal officials and civic leaders have contributed to the enlargement and refinement of my views about the urban university. I wish especially to acknowledge the friendly suggestions and helpful criticisms made by my colleagues in the Department of Urban Affairs who carefully read the manuscript and whose assistance was of immeasurable benefit to me.

Finally a word of appreciation is due the people in my office who suffered through many revisions of the manuscript without complaint and to my wife, Roberta, whose boundless and persistent encouragement kept me at the task when the many responsibilities of administration could easily have discouraged or postponed this effort.

J. MARTIN KLOTSCHE

University of Wisconsin–Milwaukee
October 1965

A Profile of the Urban University

IF A PREDICTION HAD BEEN MADE IN 1900 THAT UNIVERSITIES located in urban centers would by mid-century be enrolling almost one-half of the students in degree-granting institutions, as well as providing for several million adults on a part-time basis a wide assortment of credit and noncredit courses, such comments would have been labeled ridiculous. If the further comment had been made that use by students of private automobiles would necessitate massive land acquisitions on every urban campus for parking areas, such an observation would have been dismissed as equally preposterous. If, further, it had been suggested that universities in cities would be educating not only doctors, lawyers, and ministers, but also engineers, pharmacists, nurses, accountants, managers, architects, and social workers, the charge would have been made that the university had deserted its true purpose.

Yet all this happened. Large in size and complex in structure, our urban universities today represent a major segment of American higher education, enroll large numbers of students, and offer a varied educational fare. Burgeoning enrollments are making increasingly heavy demands on the resources of the university and community while the demands of society for a larger pool of trained manpower compel them to engage in instruction, research, and public service functions unheard of a generation ago. Nor is the end in sight. Existing institutions will continue to expand, new ones will come into being, and all will be subjected to the increasing pressures of a society that demands a higher level of educational achievement of its people.

The emergence of the urban university in America is relatively recent. Our early colleges were located in the countryside and this pastoral image has persisted. In Europe, on the other hand, the university tradition has been strikingly urban. Many of Europe's universities originated in medieval towns such as Bologna and Paris, and in more recent times, in such cities as London, Manchester, Berlin, Hamburg, Frankfurt, Milan, and Brussels.

The University of Paris, for example, has always been in and of the city. Early it drew its students from all parts of the Western world, while such great teachers as Abelard made Paris not only a vital intellectual center but also a hotbed of controversy and disputation. Town and gown conflicts were frequent. So bitter did the feeling become in the thirteenth century that the university closed its doors. Its scholars went elsewhere, to return only after they were guaranteed full independence and adequate protection to carry on their work.

In Italy, too, cities vied with each other not only for leadership in commerce, literature, and the arts, but also for universities. Bologna took drastic measures to prevent other cities from bidding for its professors. The death penalty was decreed for anyone who entered into a conspiracy to transfer the university to another city. Similar punishment was meted out to any professors who left Bologna to lecture elsewhere.[1]

This inclination to locate Europe's universities in cities continued into the modern period. In Britain, in spite of the opposition of Cambridge and Oxford, and in protest against the religious tests imposed for entry there, the University of London was established early in the nineteenth century. Provincial universities were founded in the emerging industrial centers of England later in that century and at the beginning of the present. The dramatic development of German universities in the nineteenth century, with strong emphasis on science and public administration, was due in part to their location in cities where political activity was concentrated and where a technological emphasis was developing.[2]

Notable exceptions to this urban tradition were Oxford and Cambridge. In flight from the harassments of Paris, scholars in the twelfth century chose a provincial town rather than a city. They thus moved through London and on to Oxford where "the advantage of university dominance of a small town was clearly superior to city dominance of the university."[3] Not only did the location of universities at Oxford and Cambridge have far-reaching effects on their development and character, but the Oxford and Cambridge way, rather than the urban model prevalent on the European continent, also conditioned the development of American higher education during its early period.

It was inevitable that American institutions would follow the collegiate pattern of Oxford and Cambridge. Frederick Rudolph suggests that

the development of the English pattern in the New World was not simply a conscious effort to adapt the collegiate system to American circumstances. It was at first the only solution to the absence of large concentrations of population. Not to have the collegiate way would have required cities—cities that could offer up sufficient numbers of students attracted to the college from a surrounding countryside. In the absence of cities and knowing the English pattern, the founders of Harvard and other colonial colleges naturally subscribed to the collegiate way. By the time that the colleges in Philadelphia and New York were under way, the collegiate pattern was not a necessity, for there were cities. But by then what had been a necessity had become a tradition, and from then on the founders of American colleges either adhered to the tradition or clumsily sought a new rationale.[4]

The urban university, if defined in broad terms as one located in and serving an urban community, had to await the evolution of the metropolis to emerge as a major force in American higher education. Thus urban institutions were conspicuously absent from the educational scene when our society was predominantly rural. But as cities grew, universities located in them became increasingly aware of their urban environment. At the same time new institutions were established in other cities to make educational opportunities available to the many.

As a matter of course, then, large cities preceded the urban university in time. New York City, with a population of three and one-half million people in 1900, had as its largest institution Columbia University with an enrollment of only 2,452. Chicago, with slightly over one and one-half million people, had the University of Chicago with 3,174 students. These cities were followed by Philadelphia (population 1,293,697) with the University of Pennsylvania (enrollment 645), and Boston (population 650,892) with Harvard University (enrollment 4,103). Of the ten largest cities in the United States in 1900, only four had universities with enrollments in excess of 2,000.

Urban universities, then, as we know them today were nonexistent at the beginning of the century. But this was all to change in the next few decades. By 1924, of 913 colleges reporting to the Commissioner of Education, 145 or about 15 per cent were located in cities of 100,000 or over. These 145 institutions enrolled more than 40 per cent of all college students in the United States. By 1930, of those institutions reporting an enrollment in excess of 15,000, all were located in cities with a population of 600,000 or more. The list was headed by City College of New York, with 35,189 students; in 1900 it had reported only 1,694 students. Of the eighteen institutions in 1930 with 10,000 or more students, all were in cities with a population of at least 500,000, except the University of Illinois, the University of Michigan, and the University of Wisconsin.

Much of this growth in urban university enrollments occurred from 1920 to 1930. At the beginning of that decade the twenty largest institutions in the United States, in addition to the three just mentioned, included Ohio State University, the University of Nebraska, the State University of Iowa, Cornell University, the

University of Texas, and the University of Missouri, none of them located in a large metropolitan area. But in the next ten years the shift to the large urban university assumed major proportions. Notable in that decade, for example, was the growth of City College of New York, from 4,573 to 35,189 students; New York University, from 12,867 to 33,101; Temple University, from 7,748 to 11,169; Hunter College, from 3,457 to 10,279, and the University of Pittsburgh, from 5,405 to 11,886. S. P. Capen, upon his inauguration as chancellor of the University of Buffalo, wrote in 1923 that

cities are now taking the lead in the national industry of building universities. If anyone doubts this statement, let him run over in his mind the great cities of the country and note what has happened and is happening to the institutions located in or near them . . . Forces are at work behind this movement that are as irresistible as natural law.[5]

The growth of the urban university assumed dramatic proportions in the post-World War II era. Today, every city in the United States with a population of more than 500,000 has at least one urban university of substantial size. Some have two, three, or even more, as in the case of New York City, Chicago, Los Angeles, and Philadelphia, while every city with a population between 200,000 and 500,000—there were 41 such cities in 1960—now has a degree-granting institution of higher learning that is broadly based in its enrollments and its program.

That the growth of the urban university is likely to be even more explosive in the future seems self-evident. Ours is an increasingly urban society. As the number of those seeking to attend college grows, and as a larger percentage of students comes from the lower-middle and lower income levels of society, the pressures for entrance into urban universities will be intensified. Rising tuition charges and high entrance requirements are dramatically cutting down the number of students from low income families able to attend many institutions, despite larger scholarship funds and organized efforts to equalize opportunity. With the costs of education constantly mounting, more young people will, therefore, find it necessary to remain at home while attending college.

Publicly supported colleges and universities will have to bear an increasing share of the responsibility for providing expanded education, as will the community colleges and the technical institutes. Public urban universities especially will be subjected to increased pressures to provide higher education for young people who, because of financial hardships, would otherwise be denied it. For this reason state universities, not originally located in what are now the major urban concentrations of their states, are moving into the cities with major university developments. The establishment of the University of Wisconsin-Milwaukee in 1956 as a second major campus of the University of Wisconsin, and the creation of a new campus for the University of Illinois in Chicago, are examples of the efforts of state universities to identify themselves with the educational requirements of an urban age. Developments in Baltimore, Kansas City, New Orleans, St. Louis, Cleveland, Houston, Buffalo, Wichita, Boston and Portland further reflect the increasing concern of governing boards and university administrators to meet the educational needs of urban America.

These events will lead to the reversal of a major trend in American higher education. Bringing university education to people where they live will provide for many a chance to become educated with a minimum of financial sacrifice. Thus the urban university can become the capstone of American higher education bringing reality to the ideal that all should be educated to the limit of their talent and capacity. If we are to reach what Dr. James B. Conant has called "the untapped reservoir of high ability," the urban university will have to assume a larger share of that responsibility. If intelligence susceptible of training is our most valuable resource, and is to be found at all levels, then the search for it everywhere, but especially among the disadvantaged, could well result in a significant discovery of undeveloped talent, at present being lost but essential to the future of our nation's welfare. Thus as the state and land-grant universities in the past provided major opportunity for the children of middle income families, so the urban university, especially the publicly supported one, can bring to realization the educational aspirations of America's lower income families. To meet this requirement the urban university must assume a vigorous role in tapping reservoirs of ability.

To define an urban university is not an easy task. Nor is there a satisfactory method of accurately determining the number of urban universities in America. The Association of Urban Universities estimated in 1960 that there were approximately 200, enrolling about one-half of all the students in degree-granting institutions. The number would be somewhat smaller if the urban university is defined as one located in a metropolitan area, offering graduate or professional training at least at the level of the master's or second professional degree, and concerned in outlook and program with its urban environment. In any event, urban universities enroll a substantial portion of our total college population and are growing more rapidly than their nonurban counterparts.

The diversity that has characterized American higher education generally applies to institutions in large cities as well. Over the years our colleges and universities developed independently and autonomously. The result has been a highly diversified and decentralized growth, with wide variations in size, outlook, pattern of organization, educational framework, student body, and financial support.[6]

The Association of Urban Universities, for example, includes in its membership this country's oldest university, Harvard, but also some of our newest institutions, such as some of the colleges in the City University of New York, and Roosevelt University in Chicago. In the urban group are private and public (municipal and state), denominational and independent, and technical as well as multipurpose institutions. They range from enrollments of only a few thousand to over 35,000. They are to be found in every part of the country—Akron, Baltimore, Boston, Chicago, Cincinnati, Detroit—and on through the alphabet, wherever there is a metropolitan area. Some limit enrollments drastically; others are non-selective. Some are prestigious, with worldwide reputation. Others are limited to the immediate area they serve.

Yet a pattern does emerge. The earliest urban institutions of higher learning in America were either privately or municipally controlled. Only recently have state universities begun to play an increasingly important role in metropolitan communities.

The privately endowed urban universities fall into several categories. Some, national in character and now located in heavy urban concentrations, were founded when our society was agrarian, but were significantly influenced by the urbanization of the late nineteenth and twentieth centuries. Notable in this group are Harvard University, founded in 1636; Yale University, in 1700; the University of Pennsylvania, in 1740, and Columbia University in 1754.

Another group, founded after the American Revolution and often located on the edge of a city, were equally influenced by the urban environment. As they grew, so did the cities in which they were located. In this category are University of Pittsburgh (1787), George Washington University (1821), Western Reserve University (1826), New York University (1831), Tulane University of Louisiana (1834), Boston University (1839), University of Buffalo (1846), University of Rochester (1850), Washington University (1853), Johns Hopkins University (1867), Syracuse University (1870), Vanderbilt University (1872), University of Southern California (1880), Temple University (1884), and University of Chicago (1890). The establishment of such private institutions in urban areas had virtually ceased by the end of the nineteenth century, with some notable exceptions such as the University of Miami (1921), Long Island University (1926), Fairleigh Dickinson University (1941), and Roosevelt University (1945).

The private denominational institution, on the other hand, had a different pattern of development. Of the Protestant institutions of higher learning established in the nineteenth and early twentieth centuries, few were located in cities. There were some exceptions, such as American University (1893) and Southern Methodist University (1911), but for the majority an urban location was contrary to the spirit and intent of their founders. To them, a secluded hamlet or the prairie was more likely to safeguard the morals of the young than the city with its distractions and corruptions. Thus a pastoral setting for many of America's denominational colleges was natural and inevitable. That such a secluded atmosphere might cut students off from the main currents of life was not considered a handicap.

Early Catholic colleges showed little preference for the cities. By the late nineteenth century, however, urbanization was determining the location of some. As a result, by the end of the century the Catholic urban institution was much more common. This was especially true of Jesuit institutions. The Jesuits followed the advice of their founder, St. Ignatius, and often located their colleges in cities where the greatest concentrations of Catholics were.[7]

Still another type of urban institution, privately financed and controlled, is the technical institute. Its emergence in the nineteenth century was a result of the rapid industrialization of the United States and the failure of existing colleges to reflect the educational changes demanded by an industrial society. Rensselaer Polytechnic Institute, located in Troy, New York, was founded in 1824. The establishment of the Massachusetts Institute of Technology in 1865 gave further impetus to the technical institute movement by providing a full course of scientific instruction and laboratory experience for prospective engineers and technicians.

By 1900 there were over forty such technical institutes in the United States. A select number have gained national prominence. Most notable is the Massachusetts Institute of Technology, one of the great scientific centers of the world. No longer a technical institute in the narrow sense of the word, its program includes not only science and engineering, but also urban planning, industrial management, international studies, and the humanities and social studies. Among other technical institutions that qualify as urban universities are the Carnegie Institute of Technology, Pittsburgh;

Case Institute of Technology, Cleveland, and the Illinois Institute of Technology, Chicago.

As early as 1869 Charles W. Eliot identified the importance of locating the technical institute in an urban setting. He concluded that

a technological school is best placed in a large city in a great industrial center within easy reach of works, mills, forges, machine shops, and mines. The professors of a scientific school have need to be brought into daily contact with practical affairs, to watch the progress of new inventions as they develop from day to day, and to know the men who are improving special industries. The students of a scientific school have a like need.[8]

Dr. James R. Killian, formerly president of the Massachusetts Institute of Technology, described the relationship between the technical institute and its community as symbiotic, the two living together in intimate association and capitalizing on its many advantages.[9] The specialized urban libraries, laboratories, and facilities, supplementing those of the institution, offer the scholar unusual opportunities for research and investigation. A wide variety of professional societies give faculty members opportunity to associate with persons of similar interest. Occasions for consultation enable faculty members to offer their professional services to the industry of the area, while specialists employed in industry provide a valuable pool of part-time instructors upon which the institution can draw.

For the student attending the technical institute there are also advantages in its being located in the city. A cooperative educational program with alternate periods spent on campus and in industry has been effectively developed in many places as a means of combining theoretical knowledge with practical experience. In addition, part-time employment in a field in which the student is concentrating is readily available in any metropolitan community. Similarly, a career choice may be facilitated by the wide variety of opportunities within the metropolitan area.

For the community, the resources provided by a technical institute located in its midst are substantial. Industry depends heavily upon personnel trained at such centers, and finds recruitment much easier when the institutions are nearby. Refresher courses and high level mid-career programs keep its personnel on top of things in specialized and advanced fields that are constantly changing. Research and development also bring the community and the technical institute together in the development of industrial parks and research centers.

For these reasons the president of Illinois Institute of Technology concluded that a technological institution

is at home in an urban environment and that the urban environment is the ideal place for such an institution. . . . The urban community has a great deal to contribute to the technological institution, and the institution can contribute an equal amount to the growth and welfare of the community.[10]

The municipal university, defined as one supported by local taxation and administered by a local governing board, had its origin in the nineteenth century. As urbanization proceeded, the municipal institution logically emerged as a means of meeting the needs of a more complex urban society. R. H. Eckelberry has pointed out that

from the time of the great commercial development of the later Middle Ages to the present, cities have played an increasingly important part in the life of the time. . . . The urbanization of our civilization and the increasing complexity of modern life might almost be said to be synonymous. It is in the cities especially that industrial, political, and social problems are so enormously complex that a much larger number of technically trained specialists and a more general diffusion of liberal education are necessary. It is but natural, therefore, that the people of cities have found existing educational provisions inadequate to their needs and have, by establishing municipal universities and by other means, sought to meet those needs.[11]

In 1964 there were still ten municipal institutions remaining in the United States, enrolling 161,456 students. These institutions were:

	Enrollment (Fall 1964)
City University of New York: Brooklyn (1847), City (1847), Hunter (1870), and Queens (1937) Colleges	101,040
University of Cincinnati (1819)	22,561
Municipal University of Omaha (1908)	8,408
University of Toledo (1872)	9,013
University of Akron (1870)	8,832
University of Louisville (1789)	7,375
Washburn University of Topeka (1865)	4,227

Source: Garland G. Parker, "Statistics of Attendance in American Universities and Colleges, 1964–1965," *School and Society*, January 9, 1965.

No new municipal universities have been established in recent years; nor is it likely that any will be in the future. Recently, some have changed their base of financial support as well as their method of control. Thus, Wayne State University, for a long time one of the largest municipal universities in the United States, made the transition from city to county and finally to full state university status in 1959. Similarly the Municipal University of Wichita, established in 1926, became as of July 1, 1964, Wichita State University. Enabling legislation has recently been passed by the Ohio legislature to permit state status for both the University of Akron and the University of Toledo. The City University of New York, established in 1961 to provide a coordinated university system for New York City, now receives substantial state support for its program of teacher preparation as well as additional assistance for capital expenditures and newly established graduate programs.

The municipal university, by enabling students to live at home, makes higher education possible for many to whom it would otherwise be denied. As early as 1912, when college attendance was still the privilege of a few, a questionnaire was sent to students attending the University of Cincinnati. Of those enrolled, 61 per cent could not have attended an institution outside the city.[12] Students attending college in the city in which they live often support themselves wholly or in part, and in some cases contribute to the support of members of their family. There can be no doubt that the municipal university has contributed substantially to equalization of educational opportunity.

The great increase in the taxable property of cities during their early growth gave them an economic base to provide financial support for these municipal institutions. Today, however, that tax base is not as generous as it once was. With new demands constantly being made upon the tax dollar, the municipal university is faced with serious financial problems. As a result its ranks have dwindled. Those that remain are seeking new sources of financial support, and pressing for wider areas of representation at the county and state levels, to meet increasing demands for services and plant expansion. Confidence in their ability not only to survive but also to grow and expand has been expressed by the president of one of the municipal universities in these words:

The ranks of municipal universities have dwindled, but the remaining institutions continue to increase in size and service to ever widening areas. It can be predicted that they will continue to seek new sources of support which will result in still broader service.[13]

Last to appear on the urban scene were the state and land-grant institutions. Founded when the country was predominantly rural, they were, for the most part, located outside the large population centers of their states. Ann Arbor had fewer than 5,000 inhabitants when the University of Michigan was founded. The state's largest city at the time was Detroit with 21,019 (1850). Madison had a population of less than 1,500 at the time of the founding of the University of Wisconsin. The state's largest city, Milwaukee, had 20,061 (1850). Urbana-Champaign had fewer than 7,000 inhabitants when the University of Illinois was established. The state's largest city, Chicago, had 298,977 (1870). The story was the same in Colorado (Boulder and Denver); Ohio (Columbus and Cincinnati); Missouri (Columbia and Kansas City); Louisiana (Baton Rouge and New Orleans), and Indiana (Lafayette-Bloomington and Indianapolis). There were exceptions, in Minnesota, California, and Washington; but more often than not, state universities and land-grant institutions were not established in the most populous centers of the states.

In recent years, dramatic changes have taken place. Returning GIs, anxious to take advantage of the educational subsidy provided by the government, flocked to campuses at the conclusion of World War II. Institutions, not always able to accommodate students in existing facilities, decentralized, and often offered programs in the more populous centers of the state. Even after GI pressures had subsided, the number of applicants continued to rise sharply. As a result state universities began assuming greater responsibilities in the urban areas. In Wisconsin, for example, the legislature authorized the creation in 1956 of the University of Wisconsin-Milwaukee. Fashioned out of two existing state institutions, the Wisconsin State College and the University Extension Division, by the fall of 1965 it was enrolling almost 13,000 students, of whom more than 1,600 were graduate students. The University of Illinois campus in Chicago opened its doors in the spring of 1965. It is designed to accommodate 20,000 by 1975. A new state university was opened in Cleveland in the fall of 1965 in anticipation of a major educational development in that metropolitan area.

On August 31, 1961, the University of Buffalo, which had operated as a private university for 116 years, merged officially with the State University of New York and became the State University of New York at Buffalo. Enrolling 11,000 day and 6,000 evening students at the time of the merger, it expects shortly to have 22,500 students, of whom 15,000 will be day and 7,500 evening enrollees. In 1963 the University of Houston was incorporated into the Texas system of higher education, providing a greatly needed institution in the South's largest city. In its first year of operation as a state institution, its enrollment reached 17,430, a 25 per cent increase over the previous year. In Missouri, with the cost of education expected to treble in fifteen years, state support to meet the demand for low cost education was critical. As a result, effective July 1, 1963, the private University of Kansas City became the University of Missouri at Kansas City, in anticipation of an estimated 20,000 full-time students. Plans for a major university expansion in St. Louis also are under way.

State and land-grant institutions have established a number of extension centers in urban concentrations. In 1962, almost 150 such branches were being operated by 43 universities in 31 states.[14] In Indiana, Purdue and Indiana Universities have established centers in Fort Wayne, Hammond, Indianapolis, Michigan City, Gary, South Bend, and East Chicago. This makes it possible for over 90 per cent of high school graduates to begin college work within 25 miles of their homes. Similarly, the University of Georgia, University of Michigan, Michigan State University, State University of New Jersey, Pennsylvania State University, Rutgers, University of Tennessee, University of Virginia, and University of Wisconsin have established undergraduate campuses in one or more urban areas. In this manner, then, are the state and land-grant universities, originally located in quiet country, reversing the earlier trend in higher education in which the urban university was privately or municipally controlled.[15]

What are the distinguishing characteristics of an urban university? Institutions less urban in character tend to dominate their community in a manner not possible for a university located in a city. One-fourth of Oxford and one-fourth of Cambridge are owned by the university or its colleges, with additional university holdings of substantial size lying outside their boundaries. To be sure, many university towns are changing in character. Oxford is now a center of heavy industry, with many new activities that do not emanate from the university. Heidelberg has lost many of the features that historically characterized it as a university town. Its population has doubled in twenty years, and because of rapid industrialization it has taken on many of the aspects of a modern city. Yet such university towns as Leyden, Göttingen, and Marburg in Europe, St. Andrews and Cambridge in Great Britain, and Princeton, Ann Arbor, Urbana, and Madison in the United States have maintained their distinctive characteristics.

The urban university, in contrast, cannot be so easily identified in its larger city setting. Its real estate holdings, in relation to the total area of the city, are minimal, while a host of cultural and intellectual activities are generated by other community institutions. In 1928 Dr. Elmer Brown, chancellor of New York University, highlighted this as an asset and predicted that

in a great center of population, the university wins its eminence or pre-eminence through its interaction with a full complement of the capital institutions of modern life. It serves and is served, not as a matter of course or matter of tradition, but as an active maker of modern life. It may at times suffer eclipse because of the colossal activities that surge about it, but if it comes into its full measure of service given and received, a mighty exhilaration vibrates through its life. Therein lies the victory of urban universities at their best.[16]

In competing with other institutions in the city, an urban university can be selective and concentrate on those activities which it is best equipped to undertake and which are true to its purpose.

At the same time the city can offer a wide variety of research, cultural, and intellectual resources not found in smaller communities. Here are the great museums, the art galleries, the concert halls, the playhouses, libraries, and zoological gardens. Here the social scientist can see real rather than imaginary problems of public concern. Here the medical student has ample clinical materials. Here the engineer and scientist can relate to the dramatic developments of industrial technology, and utilize the city's industrial and research facilities. The entire urban community is a laboratory.

All urban universities, public or private, large or small, single- or multi-purpose, in blighted areas or in attractive residential sections, are struggling with their environment. Burgeoning enrollments, limited acreage, high land costs, problems of renewal and conservation, face every urban campus. John Millis, president of Western Reserve University, reported that

flight from the center of the city, the decay of the city, the encroachment of population, pressure for land and competition for land, the progress of the automobile upon our streets, if possible, are all problems common to the urban situation. They are therefore problems of an urban university, and of those who have the responsibility of managing those institutions, and particularly of those who have the responsibility of planning the future of our institutions.[17]

Some urban institutions have solved their problems by moving elsewhere. A few, more fortunate than most, have adequate campuses or are located adjacent to park lands or other public areas that offer chance for growth. But for most institutions such opportunities do not exist. An already tremendous investment discourages a move elsewhere. Nor is it always to the institution's best interest to relocate even though land in abundance is available. President Gaylord Harnwell of the University of Pennsylvania suggested that

although vistas of greenery and rolling hills have a certain nostalgic appeal, contact with one's fellows has always been the greatest stimulus that man experiences; we are truly urbanites in an urban age, living together in a degree of propinquity and comfort that was not and indeed could not have been achieved before our generation.[18]

Actually, most urban universities have no choice but to make the best of their location, acquiring additional land in adjacent areas, often at great expense and effort, encouraging high density use of existing properties, and participating in a variety of ways in the revitalization, rehabilitation, and conservation of their area.

The nature of the student body influences the character of many urban universities. "Streetcar college," "subway university," and "blue shirt institution" convey a not always accurate description of institutions located in big cities. The commuting student who is "half in and half out, half at college and half at home" is common among undergraduates. This is true even of some of the older prestige institutions. For example, at Columbia College, half the undergraduates were recently reported as residents of New York City, while 75 per cent of the undergraduate students at Johns Hopkins were reported as coming from Baltimore. Even at Harvard, 30 per cent of a recent freshman class lived within 20 miles of Cambridge.[19]

Since a large proportion of the undergraduate student body in an urban university comes from the lower income levels of society, jobs are important as a means of meeting educational costs and making college education available to those who strongly want it. The lower educational attainment of parents causes them to underestimate the value of a college education and forces many students to rely on their own resources to finance educational costs.

The adult continuing student is also an important element of the urban university. Often part-time, he must take his university work in the evening. Of the 87 institutions of the Association of Urban Universities reporting enrollments in the fall of 1963, 14 enrolled over 60 per cent of their student body as part-time, 18 had at least 50 per cent enrolled on a part-time basis, 47 had between 25 and 50 per cent part-time enrollments, while only eight had less than 25 per cent of their student body in this category.

Such evening offerings are now a standard listing in urban university catalogues, reflecting the strong desire of many to continue their formal education. Full-time employees seeking to gain promotion in their companies, advanced professionals wanting to keep current in their own area of specialization, housewives released from the responsibilities of preschool children, and citizens who simply want to satisfy some special interest are coming to urban universities in great numbers.

These adult offerings are unquestionably one of the distinctive characteristics of the urban university. Universities less urban in their setting have also developed programs for adults, but rarely have they constituted a major educational effort. Often, adult education is considered of secondary concern. Teachers are assigned who have little enthusiasm for it and who have no sympathy for the special requirements of the adult. Budgetary support is often lacking, since faculties and administrators resist commitment of funds for this purpose at the expense of other programs. The public relations value or the income-producing potential of the program often carries more weight than its educational value. Donald McNeil put his finger on the problem when he stated: "But let the issue be in terms of allocating cold cash and warm bodies of faculty members to the institution's continuing education program, and actions become weaker than a thousand words."[20]

Yet with advances in technology, increased specialization, and additional leisure time, the urban university will have to make greater commitments in this field. It will require not only allocation of resources but also a clear understanding of its appropriate role. The urban university is peculiarly subject to many community pressures in the area of professional and continuing education. This stems in part from its own evolution. Many urban universities have absorbed existing professional and vocational institutions in the community. Proprietary institutions, failing to be accredited or encountering financial difficulties, have often willingly joined forces with a well established, growing university.

As a result the urban university must resist those demands not true to the purpose for which it exists—the advancement of learning. That there is an intimate and close relationship between the university and its community no one will deny. Yet no university should sacrifice its primary goal in pursuit of community approbation. It should at all times seek to be respected rather than to be popular. As Henry Steele Commager has written:

. . . the first responsibility of the university is not to serve its immediate community but to serve the much larger community of learning of which it is a part . . . those urban universities that resolutely act on this principle are also those that command the most ardent and generous support from their communities—London and Paris, let us say, or Harvard and Columbia and Johns Hopkins. The first purpose of the university is not to serve the practical and vocational needs of the local community . . . but to serve the needs of society at large and in the realms of basic research. It is reassuring that the universities which act on this principle are those which, in the end, enjoy both affection and prestige.[21]

No theme in American higher education has been repeated with greater frequency and more emphasis in recent years than that of the unprecedented growth and expansion facing our colleges and universities. Enrollments will continue to soar. The doubling of enrollments often stated as probable in the next decade may prove to be conservative. There will be more people of college age, and a larger proportion of them will be attending college. Another influential force has been described by Sidney Tickton as "the effect that automation and mechanization are having on the number of jobs available for young people in our economy. . . . They have to be greeted with something better than a rejection mechanism, unemployment, or various 'make work' activities. There has to be something better and there is—education beyond the high school."[22]

In this framework, the future of the urban university seems assured even though its role has not been fully defined. It will need to seek out talent. Few universities in our big cities have attracted to their campuses large numbers of culturally and economically deprived young people with potential ability. The record, in fact, is unimpressive. Yet here is an unparalleled chance for the urban university to contribute to the major assault that must be made on inequality of educational opportunity, and thereby gain acceptance as public policy that the only legitimate limitation is the individual's ability.

But beyond the requirement of enlarging this base, demands are increasing that education be continued for a longer period of a person's life than has been the case. Continuing learning has become a vital element in every individual's growth, and is already an essential element in today's educational revolution. Peter Drucker has suggested that the education of adults may well become America's major "growth industry." Programs catering to adults are therefore not only legitimate concerns of the urban university, but essential for it to develop if it intends to respond to the needs of an increasingly complex social system. Urban universities must give more than lip service to this effort. Nothing short of a total commitment will suffice.

It is to identify the special character of the urban university and to suggest the role it can play in America that this volume has been written. Its mission in American higher education has not yet been properly identified, nor has it taken its rightful place in the educational councils of the nation. In large part the responsibility for this failure falls on the institutions themselves. The identification of a university as urban has often been taken as a heavy handicap in the development of a quality program. Sensitive to its low estate, the urban university frequently conceives of itself as dispensing a kind of educational charity and giving a minimum of education to those who can afford no better. Henry Heald has suggested that the urban university possesses certain shortcomings that do not limit older and more residential universities. These might be described as

a relatively late start; inadequate prestige; a group of alumni from whom it is not easy to raise substantial financial support; and a state of mind. The state of mind seems to me to be the most important factor. . . . Too often it is an attitude preoccupied with the darker elements in the situation; defensive, not infrequently apologetic; oriented more toward the avoidance of failure than the affirmative realization of large possibilities and high hopes.[23]

The urban university is on the threshold of an unparalleled growth. More students will be knocking at its doors. Increasing demands will be made of it in the areas of teaching, research, and service. With our society rapidly becoming urbanized, it should especially be challenged by its urban location and by the unique role it can play in contributing to the quality of urban life.

CHAPTER II

The University and the Urban Scene

THE UNIVERSITY LOCATED IN THE CITY MUST HAVE A DEEP CON-
cern about the urban process, and use its resources to influence the
character of urban life. Henry Steele Commager stated, in capsule
form, the challenge offered to every university in America located
in a metropolitan community in these terms:

If our universities are to enjoy the advantages of their urban position,
if they are to be to American society what the great urban universities
of Europe have been to their societies, they must assume responsibility
for the development of urban and regional civilization. . . . What they
need is an awareness of their opportunities and potentialities; what they
need is a philosophy.[1]

That many urban universities have not accepted this challenge does
not detract from the validity of the statement. It simply underscores
the need for a more careful examination of the role the urban
university can play in American society. For the university located
in the metropolis is at the very center of the most dynamic and
volatile force in America today.

In a little more than a century, the United States has been trans-
formed from a predominantly agricultural society into the most
highly industrialized nation in the world. There has been a dou-

bling of the percentage of America's city population every 50 years. In 1800, 5 per cent of the nation's population lived in urban communities; by 1850, it was 15 per cent; by 1900, 39 per cent, and by 1950, 64 per cent. During the nineteenth century the urban population of the United States grew from 210,873 people living in six cities to 18,284,385 living in 448 cities.[2]

This trend toward urbanization has been even more evident in recent times. In 1960 approximately 70 per cent of the population was urban, while five American cities—New York, Chicago, Los Angeles, Philadelphia, and Detroit—accounted for 20 per cent of the nation's total population. Our population in the ten-year period 1950–1960 increased by 18 per cent. But in the same period the urban population increased by nearly 30 per cent, while the rural population decreased by a fraction of 1 per cent. Eighty-four per cent of the increase occurred in the 212 standard metropolitan areas. These metropolitan areas showed a 26 per cent increase in population, while the population of the rest of the country increased by only 7 per cent. Our urban population increased in all 50 states of the Union; in four states it doubled. In contrast, the rural population declined in 28 states.

The extent of the concentration of population in metropolitan areas becomes even more evident when seen in relation to land area. Urbanized areas—that is, the central city and the urban fringe—represent only 0.7 per cent of the total land area of the United States, yet contain over 50 per cent of the nation's inhabitants. Here the population per square mile is 183 times that of non-metropolitan U. S., while in the central cities it is 261 times as high.[3]

This urbanization is certain to continue. The United States Bureau of the Census predicts a population of 220 million by 1975. The Urban Land Institute of Washington, D.C., predicts that by the year 2000, 85 per cent of the country's 320 million people will be living in urban areas. Such growth, it reports, would require a land area of 55,000 square miles, or seven times that of the State of New Jersey. It further predicts that there will be 10 supercities containing one-third of our total population, with a 450-mile strip of continuous metropolitan flow from Boston to Washington, containing a population of 31 million; an "industrial Riviera" stretching from Gary, Indiana, around Chicago and into Wisconsin, with 8.5 million people; and a recreational and retirement belt stretching from Jacksonville to Miami, containing 3 million people.[4]

Two-hundred and seventy-five million people living in our urban areas by the year 2000! This, indeed, is staggering.

One example of the complexities of our urban system is the many jurisdictions. A recent survey showed over 16,000 separate units of local government in our metropolitan areas, with an average of 96 jurisdictions per area. Traffic congestion continues unabated, with the Bureau of Public Roads predicting 40 million more motor vehicle registrations by 1973, an increase of 75 per cent over present figures. We have more than 14 million people living in houses beyond rehabilitation, and additional millions in sub-standard homes. Our central cities contain large areas of blight, with ghettos often hemming in minority groups. Large numbers of our city people live in poverty, outside the main stream of life. Land adjacent to metropolitan centers is being swallowed up at the rate of a million acres a year. Our air and water are polluted. Endless time and energy are devoted to going to and from work by those living in the suburbs.

Cities are more than a collection of statistics. More than houses, streets, automobiles, factories and industries, shopping centers, stores, and parking lots, cities are a human habitat in which man is trying somehow to come to terms with his environment. They are focal points of learning as well as centers of religious and cultural life. They are important points of trade, production, and transportation, as well as the source of remunerative employment. Cities also represent conflict, accommodation, and common civic tasks that need to be performed. Concern over our cities involves more than simply striving to improve transportation, to relieve traffic congestion, to mount urban renewal programs, to sanitize water, and to purify the air. It involves a community consciousness that seeks to create a climate to resolve some of the more urgent problems of the city and in the process improve urban life.

The central domestic issue of our times revolves around the problems of our metropolitan areas. The population explosion, the heavy concentration of people in our cities, central city growth and decay, the flight to the suburbs, the industrial, commercial, and retail dispersion to areas outside the inner core, and the all-pervasive influence of the automobile illustrate the point with dramatic force. Harrison E. Salisbury has observed that the greatest revolution in progress today is taking place in the cities and suburbs of the United States. He sees it as a "heedless movement whose catalytic agents are social mutation and technological change—and its symptoms are big-city decay, rural blight, and spongelike population cancers spreading remorselessly along the arteries of the great motorcar routes."[5]

Clearly many of these problems are already well ahead of our best efforts to deal with them. We are approaching an urban crisis, with the minor ripples of the past giving way to tidal waves that could engulf our cities unless solutions are found. Dr. Luther Gulick contends that since "the whole mechanism of community life and executive direction, programing and planning, is behind the times now, and is totally unprepared to face the future. . . . we need new community machinery, new community thinking, new community leaders, and new powers of local government."[6] Certainly the present disordered and highly industrialized society has failed to produce the insights necessary to deal successfully with the complexities of urban concentration.

There are some who suggest that the metropolis, because it no longer seems viable, will soon be obsolete. Yet no one seriously believes that the urban trend can be reversed. A society that is based on science and technology is inevitably urban. Nor is all lost. Those who contend that the city is doomed fail to understand its historic role. Western civilization has been a civilization of cities. The very origin of the word "city" suggests that it has been the generator of civilization and a special instrument for preserving and transmitting our cultural heritage. Our cities are here to stay, and can become not only repositories of good things, centers of innovation and enterprise, but also a symbol of life itself.

That the university has a role to play in this regard needs to be fully explored, for "urban prospects in the United States . . . depend not on secession of scholarly activity but on its intensification in new directions of inquiry and investigation."[7] Certainly universities have a compelling responsibility to identify themselves with the social forces of urban America. There is much in the tradition of the American university that supports this position. Among commonly accepted tasks of institutions of higher learning have been those associated with the needs of a changing society. As the requirements and responsibilities of society have shifted, universities have provided the intellectual leadership. They have consistently played a decisive role in advancing the cause of democracy and serving the needs of a dynamic society without jeopardizing their essential mission—that of transmitting, cultivating, and advancing learning. As Fred Harvey Harrington, president of the University of Wisconsin, has aptly said: "The university is a central unit in modern culture. . . . It is the gate to life and leadership in this land. . . . There is no doubt about it. The university in America can change the world and often does."[8] Every aspect of life in America is being touched by our universities —government, agriculture, industry, labor, the performing arts, overseas activities. They are also moving into our cities with research and training programs and establishing there centers for social action.

No development in American higher education better illustrates the use of intellectual leadership to meet the needs of society than the land-grant system. Designed to provide the means by which the welfare of a rapidly expanding nation could be advanced, land-grant institutions deliberately set out, with spectacular success, to educate people, to develop programs, and to carry on research in such areas as agriculture and engineering. As a result, no other nation has approached the American record of agricultural productivity. At the beginning of this century, for example, one-third of our labor force was needed to produce food. Today, less than 10 per cent of our labor force is needed. In the Soviet Union, a farmer produces only enough to feed himself and four other people. In contrast, here a farmer produces enough to sustain himself and twenty-four others.[9] The technological and scientific revolution in agriculture has, of course, produced problems of sizable dimension. Not only has it created a problem of abundance which we have not yet satisfactorily solved, but it has also resulted in a steady and continuous decline in our rural population, with the resulting migration of people into the cities causing many new problems. Yet the record of expanded agricultural productivity has been impressive, and our universities have been central in making this possible.

Urbanism as an area of major concern has not yet had the same attention. Historically, the intellectual climate of America has not always been receptive to the urban scene. Morton and Lucia White have concluded that the growing urbanization of our society in the nineteenth century did not result in the intellectuals of that day expressing deep concern or strong affection for the city.[10] Instead, because many of our great thinkers expressed deep hostility toward urban life in America, we developed no tradition of attachment to the city. An examination of some 6,000 volumes of verse published between 1876 and 1905 brought Robert Walker to the same conclusion. While some poets found circumstances in the city to praise, generally they "constructed a myth of the city formidable in its detail and frightening in its intensity. . . . Against the small voice of those who found items to praise in the relentless rise of the city was raised the deafening plaint of the urban detractors. . . . They scored the town for its unhealthy ugliness, for its example of economic inequities, for its affinities with crime, drunkenness, sexual excesses, amorality, and artificiality."[11] There were, then, few spokesmen writing in behalf of the city and creating a climate of understanding about it.

Nor have our universities fully seen the possibilities of dealing in depth with the complexities of urban concentration. Frequently their interest has been peripheral rather than central, superficial rather than fundamental. Charging that "the university itself seems afraid of propagating ideas, of challenging accepted beliefs, of involving itself in the actual life of the larger community," Sydney Harris concluded that "if universities cannot intellectualize their neighborhoods, at least to some degree, then their influence on the social current is negligible, and their pretension to significance is absurd."[12]

While there have been islands of academic inquiry into the urban field, there has been nothing to parallel the exhaustive study of American agriculture that has characterized university endeavor during the past hundred years. A comparable effort in depth and breadth in the urban field still needs to be made. To be identified as a scholar in the field of urban affairs "was, until quite recently, equivalent to having an epitaph placed on an otherwise promising academic career."[13] Yet a minor revolution in urban scholarship is now beginning to take place, not in any way comparable to efforts in the natural sciences, or agriculture and engineering, but nevertheless impressive and encouraging.

The failure to gain approval of the urban field as a proper area of university concern should, however, not be viewed with too much dismay. Again the agricultural parallel is relevant. Agricultural research and experimentation have been eminently successful, yet they were not always embraced without reservation. Initially, popular support was not always forthcoming, and many farmers opposed efforts to establish institutions specializing in agricultural pursuits. Distrustful of the assistance offered by colleges, farmers often viewed such moves with suspicion and contempt. In the academic community, too, skepticism and hostility were expressed. The older, well established institutions charged that the newly created "cow colleges" were prostituting the cause of education in introducing vocational training at the college level. It was argued that the traditional function of training doctors, lawyers, and ministers should not be modified to include farmers and mechanics, nor should programs of agricultural studies be used to convert institutions of higher learning into cow pastures.[14] Yet, in time, the responsibility assumed by such institutions to improve agriculture and to promote the welfare of the farmer was not only accepted by the public, but demanded by it.

In like manner, it should now become a central task to understand the city, to analyze its problems, to research and comment about them, to commit university resources and to enlist those of the community so that the quality of urban life can be improved. For the insights of the humanist and philosopher, the social scientist, the scientist and engineer, and the artist can all be employed to help our cities fulfill the promise of urban living.

Because of its metropolitan location, the urban university can encourage urbanism as an appropriate field of study. Often it has been reluctant to pursue this task aggressively. Preoccupied with the problems of its own neighborhood, and slavishly imitating the pattern of the more residential college, it has often overlooked its own assets.[15]

The urban university must not, however, become so committed to the affairs of the city that the purposes for which it exists will be compromised. There is always the danger that a university can become too immersed in the problems of its community. It would indeed be fatal to its historic mission were problem solving and local politics to become its primary goals. Implied in the term "urban university" is a quality of cosmopolitanism and sophistication that makes it a part of the city while it remains apart from it. This is what has made many of the urban universities of Europe great. America's urban universities, too, must be national and world serving, their faculties in touch with like-minded scholars everywhere and their view broad rather than provincial, inclusive rather than narrow. Though local in habitation, their influence must be far-flung, bringing to their communities the knowledge and understanding not only of their region, but of the nation and the world.

The university's central role should always be that of guardian of the old and discoverer of the new. It should not be expected, as Professor Michael Oakeshott of the London School of Economics once feared, "to move step by step with the world, at the same speed, and partaking in every eccentricity of the world's fashion, refusing nothing that is offered, responsive to every suggestion."[16] The university can provide a common meeting ground for the divergent elements of the community and assist in reaching an objective understanding of its problems while at the same time providing the basis for the development of theory and policy for general application elsewhere. No community issue, whether it results from social strain, racial tension, religious conflict, nationality origin, or labor-management disagreement, should be beyond the interest of the university scholar.

A university can discharge this responsibility as no other institution can. It can examine the metropolis in its totality, seeing each problem in relationship to the whole. It can seek to identify both the shortcomings and the accomplishments of the community. It can rise above the local prejudices and see beyond the political fragmentation that characterizes our metropolitan areas. It can be a constructive critic, a standard setter, a balancing force. It can help to blaze new trails. It can stand over and above the tumult and shouting of the market place. It can speak out boldly on matters of principle, and bring clarity to community thought in a climate free of bias and emotionalism. It can seek to identify not only what is and can be, but what should be.

If diversity is the dominant characteristic of American higher education, then the urban university should embrace its special location. If it finds strength in its urban setting, and capitalizes on it, then its true mission can be accomplished. This point has been repeatedly underscored by Fred Harvey Harrington, president of the University of Wisconsin. In laying down appropriate guidelines for the development of the Milwaukee campus of the university he has said that the urban university of tomorrow "should be ready to move forward along new lines—to experiment, to generate and try out original ideas and approaches in instruction, research, and public service."[17]

The encouragement of this diversity presents a unique opportunity for some of America's newer urban universities. John Gardner in 1957 asked that we

think of American higher education as involving many different kinds of institutions, each with its significant part to play in creating the total pattern. Let us recognize that we have profited enormously by the diversity of American higher education. Let us resolve that the various kinds of institutions shall play their different roles with honor and recognition. . . . The small liberal arts college should not be afraid to remain small. The large urban institution should not be ashamed that it is large. The technical institute should not be apologetic about being a technical institute. Neither coeducational nor non-coeducational institutions should feel it necessary to explain why they are one or the other. Each institution should pride itself on the role that it has chosen to play and on the special contribution which it brings to the total diverse pattern of American higher education.[18]

What then is the special mission for the university in the urban field? It is in a position to do things that other institutions cannot. Substantial efforts to study metropolitan problems have been made by many non-university agencies. Studies made in St. Louis, Cleveland, Dayton, and New York have contributed to a better understanding of our urban society. Universities have no monopoly of expert knowledge in the urban field. Bureaus of research, metropolitan study commissions, leagues of municipalities, neighborhood associations, community councils, and civic associations have produced experts of their own who have added to the store of knowledge about our cities.

The university should not displace or in any way discourage these efforts. Rather, it needs to identify its own role. And what is that role? Teaching and research are at the center of the university's mission, and in both respects its scholars must face the facts and pursue them fearlessly. It is this impartiality and ability to meditate that enable a university to clarify the problems of the community. By presiding at the center, it can help create a climate free of bias and emotionalism.

The university can also introduce "the innovative function" into the urban field. Experimentation has been conspicuously absent from many metropolitan communities. It is often a politically inexpedient or dangerous role to play, and one which the politician and the civic leader are reluctant to assume. As a consequence, urban systems have been slow to adapt to modern requirements. Yet cities are desperately in need of new ideas, and universities, through research and experimentation, are in a strong position to provide them. Ideas can be fed into the system that will in time result in the modification and adjustment of the system to its environment.[19]

The university can also provide an over-all view of the urban scene. Compartmentalization, fragmentation, and provincialism characterize most of our metropolitan communities. Those who live in the suburbs see no reason to be concerned about the central city, while those who leave the city do not understand that their problems are not solved by moving away. In similar manner, those who remain behind have not yet grasped the inseparability of the problems of the city and those of the urban fringe. Yet such problems as smoke, water pollution, sewage, health, education, traffic and transportation, segregation and race, crime and poverty are common to all.

Many problems extend beyond the boundaries of individual cities. They are to be found in metropolitan concentrations everywhere. Large urban areas exist in all parts of the world. Everywhere there has been a metropolitan outreach with an ever widening circle of urban thrust. And everywhere great cities have been confronted with similar problems, such as the constantly increasing pressures for expanded public services, accompanied by inadequate financial resources to support such services; outdated political institutions to deal with the economic and social realities of modern urban society; a public apathy to metropolitan affairs, and an absence of imaginative, long range planning.[20]

The university comes closest to being able to identify itself with the whole of the urban scene and a total concern for the city.

For the social scientist, the philosopher, the artist, the engineer, the natural scientist through their respective disciplines can all touch every aspect of urban life—its culture, problems of sanitation and transportation, land use, its disadvantaged people in their ghettos, crime and poverty, as well as its beauty and its design.

Universities can provide a fresh point of view and devise new techniques of dealing with the increasingly complex problems of our metropolitan areas. The university should clearly be the leader and at the same time reflect the spirit of the times. In 1916, Charles Van Hise, president of the University of Wisconsin, contended that

when new and important issues are arising, when old convictions are being questioned, is a time when the men of learning, who should know the facts broadly, and who have no purpose but the greatest good of the greatest number, should be absolutely free. . . . . Times of unrest and change are not the times for the university to trim; they are the times to set every sail from the main course to the sky sails so that all may draw.[21]

While his comments were not related to the urban scene, Van Hise's view is as valid today, in a society that has become urbanized, as it was two generations ago. Yet we have only begun to nibble at the edges of the problem created by the urban thrust. On all sides there are frightening examples of the heavy price we have already paid for the neglect of our cities: blight and squalor, an urban sprawl which destroys the landscape, fragmentation of governmental units, inadequate public services, the dehumanization of our cities.

Historically, the contribution of the university to the advancement of mankind has been substantial. Its commitment to social improvement has been unmistakable. Its traditional concern for the well-being of society should now extend to the exploding metropolis. Such a university, Joseph Hudnut contended, should not be

built at the edge of a city; it should preside at the center, affirming by that relationship its leadership and serviceability. It should be conscious of its high place in the scheme of the city; conscious not of its relation to street and traffic merely, to the homes of faculty and students, to coordinated institutions and facilities, but more urgently conscious of those less immediate and less visible factors of city life, unobserved by the practical-minded, which create its usefulness as a civic force.[22]

There is, then, a unique role for our universities—that of giving new meaning to the quality of urban life.

CHAPTER III

Urban Needs and University Resources

THE NEEDS OF OUR CITIES AND THE CAPABILITIES OF OUR UNIversities to meet them can be stated as follows:

1. It has always been a major task of our universities to provide trained leadership to meet the requirements of a changing society. They should now enlarge their interest in the training of the professional and the technician to include the urban field, since a great shortage of well qualified personnel already exists and will continue to grow.

2. Knowledge about the city needs to be dramatically increased so that the quality of urban life can be improved. The university must push forward the frontiers of knowledge in the field of urban affairs.

3. The process of urbanization must be interpreted to the leadership in our metropolitan communities. The university has had a long experience in transmitting knowledge, discovered in its laboratories and libraries, into the main stream of society. The outreach of its understanding about the city into the city should be no exception.

4. A better understanding of all aspects of urban society is needed by the general public. In a democracy, intelligent and informed citizen participation is crucial.

The Municipal Year Book concluded that no single matter in 1962 had as far-reaching significance for the metropolitan scene as the recruitment, training, and retention of adequately trained manpower for tomorrow's cities.[1] The same conclusion was reached by the Municipal Manpower Commission.[2]

Specialized personnel needs have resulted in part from the rapid growth of the urban population. The need will be even greater in the future. By the end of this century, twice as many people will be living in our cities as is the case today. This concentration of people in limited living space has accelerated the demand for government service at the local level in such fields as health, safety, housing, and welfare. Demands for more and better service from local governments necessitate not only a higher level of expenditure, but an upgrading in the quality of service. Health clinics, classes for handicapped children, recreational programs, branch libraries, better police and fire protection, improved schools, more effective case work in welfare, all reflect the substantial upgrading and expanding of public services expected by people living in metropolitan areas. The need for well-trained personnel is, therefore, becoming critical.

In 1961, there were 1,734,000 persons employed by cities with populations over 10,000. This compares with 1,297,000 employed ten years earlier, or an increase of almost 35 per cent.[3] The demand for administrators and professional and technical personnel has increased even more dramatically. The Municipal Manpower Commission reported, for example, that while the population of Detroit between 1930 and 1960 rose by 6 per cent, city employment increased by 30 per cent, and the demand for administrative, professional and technical positions skyrocketed by 150 per cent. It further reported that the 212 standard metropolitan areas which now employ 230,000 persons in these specialized categories will, by 1980, need almost 400,000, or an increase of 67 per cent.[4] John Corson, chairman of the commission, identified the problem in this manner:

There may have been a time in the past when we could run our cities on the theory that any man could conduct the affairs of a municipal department even as any man might poke a fire or rock a baby, but it won't suffice for the future. Our urban areas are becoming too large and too important to the society in which we live for that kind of management and that kind of manpower.[5]

The complexities of urban life require the highly specialized services of the trained professional. Thus, aerial cartographers to assist in property assessments, geologists to advise on the number of septic tanks the soil can absorb, and computer programers to advise traffic engineers are becoming a standard requirement of the big city.[6] All of the major disciplines of a university, in fact, will soon be called upon to provide trained manpower for our cities. The urban sociologist, the demographer, the human ecologist, the public administrator, the land economist, the student of industrial relocation, transportation and marketing, the urban geographer, resource experts, legal specialists versed in land use and zoning, cultural anthropologists, and social psychologists will be needed.

The private as well as the public sector, and federal and state agencies, will be increasing demands for trained personnel. Urban problems now need to be viewed on a state-wide, regional and national basis. State and federal governments are engaged not only in extensive highway programs, but also in housing and redevelopment, air and water pollution abatement, education, vocational rehabilitation, and child welfare. Increasing attention, therefore, will have to be given to staffing these agencies.

It will not be easy to meet these manpower requirements. Municipal service has not been accorded the same level of honor as has private business, or public service at the state and national levels. Personnel officers of all major corporations rush to college campuses with flattering offerings, and hold out generous promises of promotion and recognition. Each year these efforts are intensified, with every conceivable incentive offered. In the face of such competition, local government service is at a disadvantage. The public image of the person employed by the municipality, the environment in which many public employees are forced to work, and the attitude of many municipal employees toward their own employment makes recruitment for public service at the local level difficult. The Municipal Manpower Commission's study of 1,700 local executives, for example, revealed that only 17 per cent of those interviewed would recommend a career in local government to others.[7]

Training professional personnel to meet the needs of society is not a new responsibility for our universities. Until the end of the last century, institutions of higher learning trained primarily for the learned and literary professions. But in this century they have trained business executives, labor leaders, nurses, engineers, pharmacists, social workers, and police officers. In so doing they come in contact with all segments of our national life. A close correlation now exists between the improvement of a profession and the efforts university scholars devote to advancing it. The reorientation and revolutionizing of medical education earlier in the century to include research-oriented professional training, emphasis upon the advancement of knowledge, the appointment of full-time faculty members, clinical teaching and post internships is a case in point.[8]

But educating the professional to work in the area of urban affairs has not yet reached this level of understanding and development. Harvey Perloff points out that until quite recently, education for city planning was a limited field, much of it taking place on an apprenticeship basis in the offices of planning practitioners.[9] This situation is duplicated in many other fields. Certainly we are far from supplying an adequate number of able, professionally trained people for the special tasks of an urban society. Only a few urban universities make any significant contribution to meeting the manpower needs of the local community. A survey of over 1,000 colleges and universities made by Professor Herman Berkman in preparation for the establishment of a program of urban studies at the University of Wisconsin-Milwaukee underscored the absence of such programs. A wide variety of courses related to the urban field were found to exist. Schools of public health offered courses in housing, air and water pollution; business schools advertised real estate programs; law schools gave courses in land use controls; colleges of engineering and schools of architecture gave courses in planning; graduate schools offered programs in public administration, in metropolitan affairs, and in urban science. Yet, with few notable exceptions, there were no carefully thought out, coordinated programs designed to train professional people for the urban age.

Urban universities have a major responsibility to help meet this manpower crisis. Their graduates are in many instances the very ones who will look toward public service because often they come from "social and ethnic groups which do not have as ready access to business and to certain of the professions as others, who will find in public service a social and economic mobility upward that is almost unique and who will bring . . . an understanding of some of the problems of these communities."[10] This being the case, urbanism as a service field for the young professional should appeal to the same idealism exploited so effectively in recruiting for the Peace Corps.

The urban university should develop programs that are broadly designed, intellectually valid, and that will pass the test of excellence. Harvey Perloff warns that

often new training programs are established at universities after a strong demand has developed for a certain type of knowledge and skill, and then, under pressure from harried practitioners and employers, a trade-school type program is set up. . . . It would be a cause much to be applauded if, as is not too often the case, the universities were to respond to a demand for training in relatively new and fast-growing fields by taking the initiative and evolving programs that are broadly conceived (looking to the future and not the past or present needs) and that are exciting intellectually and as high in quality as they are in ultimate practical value.[11]

The critical role for the university is more than that of providing a practical education related to a specific task. There is a desperate need not only for the professional prepared to deal with his specialty, but for versatile "gifted generalists" whose education and experience include both depth and breadth.[12] The Municipal

Manpower Commission reports, for example, that in large cities, public works directors devote no more than 5 per cent of their time to engineering matters. The greatest part of their effort is devoted to administrative matters, policy questions, and an understanding of the general urban economy.[13]

A condition, then, to be kept in mind in training the professional urbanist is the nature of society itself. Changes are occurring with such rapidity that fundamental rather than immediately practical considerations should prevail in the development of educational programs. The whole approach to urbanization problems may have to be completely recast if we are to cope successfully with them. Thus, universities should be training not for jobs that already exist, but for positions now nonexistent and surely to be needed in the future. Since it is hazardous to predict the specific occupational categories that may be needed and since considerable "lead time" is needed to train and develop talent, neither programs of a "crash" nature nor those of an immediately practical sort best serve the needs of an urban society in a state of flux. "Our most critical need a decade hence," the Rockefeller Report points out, "may be unknown today. Rather, we must prepare ourselves for a constant and growing demand for talents of all varieties, and must attempt to meet the specific needs of the future by elevating the quality and quantity of talented individuals of all kinds."[14]

To meet the crises that face our cities is as much a matter of developing a broad understanding and familiarity with many problems as it is of thoroughly mastering a specific task. To deal with the substance of policy is as important as is specific knowledge about a single problem such as water, sewage, transportation, or slums. Developing "a positive attitude toward complexity," and vigorously advocating solutions to problems that are in the public interest, can be more beneficial than concern with minutiae and detail.[15]

To meet this need the University of Wisconsin-Milwaukee established a Department of Urban Affairs in the fall of 1963. The objectives of this new graduate program were stated thus:

Contemporary society faces a growing need for a new type of specialist with broad and intensive training in the field of urban affairs. Both public and private organizations—housing and redevelopment authorities, civic associations, planning commissions, social agencies, religious institutions, industrial corporations, etc.—are becoming increasingly aware of the difficulties in solving many of their own problems without reference to the total fabric of urban life. Graduates of this pioneering program will be trained to bring the relevant knowledge and expertise of the social sciences to the solution of urban problems.[16]

Designed as an interdisciplinary program, with most of its faculty also holding appointments in other departments, its purpose is to train a new kind of specialist in urban coordination and integration. Constituting the core of the program are a seminar on the culture of cities, courses on the dynamics of metropolitan development, design of urban research, urban social structure, and the urban political process, and a capstone interdisciplinary colloquium on the city. In addition to these core courses, students take electives directed toward a particular specialty. Through such a coordinated program those training for positions in urban society will be exposed not only to general theories but also to specific fields such as transportation, housing and redevelopment, urban economics, and community development.

While training for the urban age is more properly the field of professional and graduate schools, a broad general understanding of the process of urbanization should be a part of every undergraduate's education. Undergraduate student bodies should be introduced to the new urban America and the opportunities for local career service. "The need is to enlist the interests of young people before career choices are made. The systematic impression of courses on urban affairs in college programs will inform them of career opportunities which they otherwise would not know existed."[17]

Today two out of three Americans live in metropolitan centers. By the end of the century it will be eight out of ten. Living and working in an urban-oriented society, the undergraduate student should be exposed to the broad aspects of urban culture. Here is an opportunity for the urban university to develop a general studies program using urban culture as its unifying theme. Many of man's greatest achievements have sprung from the cross-fertilization of ideas associated with urban life. Lewis Mumford has concluded that our cities have been an indispensable civilizing agency, a container, a magnet, a transformer, a force that has stimulated creativity, enlarged consciousness, and enhanced life:

Through its monuments, written records, and orderly habits of association, the city has enlarged the scope of all human activities, extending them backwards and forwards in time, and has become capable of transmitting a complex culture from generation to generation, for it marshaled together not only the physical means but the human agents needed to pass on and enlarge this heritage. That remains the greatest of the city's gifts.[18]

If the city is to fulfill its historic role as the center of culture, what better place is there to achieve an understanding of this role than in an imaginative general undergraduate program of urban studies, using the literature of urbanism to understand urbanization? A few institutions have experimented with this concept. The Dartmouth program of undergraduate education for Urban Life and Urban Affairs is significant since Dartmouth is not located in an urban environment. Yet its student body will, upon graduation, be working in many of the large metropolitan centers of America. The basic elements of the program are an introductory course on urban growth, including an international and world orientation; several special courses with urban content; cooperative arrangements among faculty members who teach courses that contain urban material; an advisory service to students and faculty; a coordinating senior seminar with opportunity for research; a system of summer internships, and a joint Dartmouth-Massachusetts Institute of Technology seminar in which students from both institutions spend a term in the Boston area. The coordinating seminar in the last year is a continuation of the introductory course on urban growth and planning and gives a view of the city as an organic whole.[19]

One of the promising efforts to bring the research potential of the university to bear on the problems of the city has come out of a suggestion by Professor Robert Wood of the Massachusetts Institute of Technology that "urban observatories" be established across the country.[20] Such observatories would be the counterpart of agricultural field stations which have successfully brought together the academic and agricultural communities. Few studies of urban problems have common designs or techniques of analysis. Results are difficult to compare, and knowledge is either not readily accessible or of limited value. By coordinating efforts under a single research plan, reliable findings in a number of areas could be made available, with officials in one city being apprised of what is being tried elsewhere.

In June 1965, the observatory idea was tested at a conference held in Milwaukee at the suggestion of Henry Maier, mayor of Milwaukee and president of the National League of Cities. In attendance were a number of mayors and urban specialists who agreed that a working relationship between city hall and halls of ivy was needed. Subsequently a network of 14 cities was designated, with willing officials and universities paired as a condition of selection.

For city leaders to state their needs to universities in this manner is a new departure in urban research. Out of this proposal may emerge a redefinition of the research function of the university, since its applied aspects will have a greater appeal to the city practitioner than the theoretical considerations associated with more traditional scholarship. In that event, the social scientist engaged in urban research will come closer to the engineer who applies theories to practical problems than to the pure scientist who is engaged in basic research.

The task of broadening the foundations of urban scholarship has just begun. Our basic knowledge of the urban scene and our understanding of the process of urbanization are still meager and inadequate. If we are to treat urban ills properly, they must be understood. To be understood, they must be studied. There is no substitute for knowledge. Diligent observation, thorough investigation, distrust of dogmatism, tentativeness of conclusion, minimum personal involvement, and reasoned skepticism—all traits of the scholar—are needed to understand the urban environment. Only with such a focus on the fundamental problems will a more satisfactory set of urban decisions be reached.

Universities, of course, are not the sole repositories of knowledge in the urban field. Market analysts and economic researchers are frequently employed by private corporations to assist in determining plant location, market, tax climate, and growth potential. Local governments depend on planning staffs to prepare studies for reaching workable solutions to problems. Special study commissions and research bureaus are amassing knowledge about the city.

These efforts are important to a better understanding of the urban scene. Yet the university scholar can make a unique contribution. Through new discoveries, confirmation of fact and theory, refinement and evaluation, he can add strands to the fabric of knowledge. The methods of experimentation, control, testing, and rejection are peculiarly suitable to an academic atmosphere. Here the scholar can conduct his investigations free from the pressures of the day. In contrast, the policy maker often needs an immediate response to complex problems. He becomes impatient when a ready solution is not available, and annoyed when additional time is needed to present alternative solutions.

Time is on the side of the university scholar. Because this is so, he can pursue basic lines of inquiry. He can doubt existing theories. He can suggest new approaches to old problems, and can inject new thrusts that would be politically unwise for the urban practitioner or policy maker to undertake. "The scientific method," the physicist P. W. Bridgman once noted, "as far as it is a method, is nothing more than doing one's damnedest with one's mind, no holds barred."[21] For this reason a university scholar engaged in urban research must be prepared to demonstrate how his views are "significantly different from or, in any sense, above and beyond what can be said by public officials, leaders of business, labor and professional organizations, churchmen, representatives of civic groups, professional consultants in almost every phase of urbanism from planning and pollution (air and water) and from traffic to taxes."[22]

Basic urban research, then, adds an element not to be found in the more applied type of investigation carried on outside university circles. With no strings attached, no time schedule, no immediate pressures, the university scholar has few limitations. Comparable to the meanderings of a dog

he acts in the dog's way, too, swinging wide, racing ahead, doubling back, covering many miles of territory that the man never traverses, all in the spirit of inquiry and the quest for truth. He leaves a crazy trail, but he ranges far beyond the genteel old party he walks with . . . . sometimes a dog runs into something in nature so arresting that not even a man can quite ignore it, and the man deviates . . . . When the two of them get home and flop down, it is . . . . the wide ranging dog who is covered with burdocks and with information of a special sort on out-of-the-way places. . . . He never feels he knows where the truth lies, but is full of rich memories of places he has glimpsed it in.[23]

The scholar can, therefore, raise questions which may be considered irrelevant or even ludicrous. Peter Rossi cites the example of a study of urban renewal in the area around the University of Chicago. It had been assumed, without serious questioning, that one of the major reasons for urban renewal was that faculty members were leaving the area in large numbers in the face of the influx of Negroes. Studies showed, however, that university personnel remained remarkably stable in their preference for Hyde Park-Kenwood as a residential area.[24] Obviously, no one with a vested interest could have been persuaded to undertake such a study. Yet "silly questions" like this do need to be raised.

Bringing perspective and balance to the urban scene is still another contribution the university scholar can make. Beyond fact finding there is need for looking at the process of "chain reaction—from situation to policy response to policy action to results—and to feed back from a survey of the results to an evaluation of the policy."[25] Those directly engaged in policy making are not always in the best position to engage in such a retrospective and evaluative process. An example of such "repercussions analysis" is a study to measure the effects of public housing in Baltimore on its residents.[26] The study was carried out at Johns Hopkins University and involved 1,000 families over a three-year period. It compared good and bad housing, and determined their effects on physical health and social adjustment. Housing and health administrators need such evaluations, either to buttress their programs or to develop alternative solutions. In the Baltimore study, a group of university scholars observed simultaneously people who had moved from a sub-standard area to newer and better housing, and a similar group who continued to live in slum conditions. It is doubtful that urban practitioners could have exploited such an opportunity with equally effective results.

Millions of dollars are being committed to rehabilitate our cities. The consequences of the redevelopment program have not yet been fully assessed, but its full purposes are not being achieved. A method of collecting data and establishing relationships between urban forms and human objectives has not yet been devised. Here, indeed, is an important task for the university scholar, operating from neutral ground, to undertake—that of providing an intellectual base for future consideration of one of the central concerns of urban America.

Antipoverty efforts offer still a further opportunity for the urban scholar. Since substantial funds will be available, universities can play a central role in the antipoverty program. There is great need for a better understanding of the nature and causes of poverty. Community agencies also need assistance in evaluating projects, in determining priorities, in defining objectives, and in having available comparative data from other urban areas. The Economic Opportunity Act of 1964 includes a provision for universities to enter into contracts with the federal government for the conduct of research, training, and demonstrations that will contribute to the objectives of the poverty program.

Practitioners and policy makers have to be concerned with the concrete needs of their particular communities. Their time and resources are limited. Their efforts must of necessity be devoted to the immediate and specific matters at hand. The university scholar, on the other hand, does not need to view his assignment in this restricted manner. Urgent practical problems need not be determining factors. He can view the various elements of the urban scene as a part of a whole and can identify relationships and cross-currents.

The fiscal crisis is a case in point. Inadequate financial resources are a chronic complaint in every American city. Not only are metropolitan communities being required to provide more services at increasing cost, but as costs mount, the city's tax base becomes more restrictive, with state and federal governments making increasing demands on the tax dollar. Our urban areas represent the greatest concentration of economic power and wealth, yet are fiscally impotent to deal with their problems. Local fiscal policy needs to be examined outside of the local framework of prejudice and tradition, and scholarly research in the field of municipal finance can do this.

The balkanization of political power is another urgent problem. Many practices at the local level are obsolete in the light of modern living and urban need. A better political and legal framework to correspond with the economic and social requirements of the twentieth century must be developed. Here are great opportunities for imagination. The researcher and fact finder can lay the groundwork for improving the structure of local government. To him, political fragmentation is to be studied rather than accepted.

In spite of the multitude of governments at the local level, an increasing number of activities of an economic and service nature cut across local jurisdictions. Many employees commute long distances to get to work. Trade and commerce are not confined to narrow political jurisdictions. Water, air, and transportation are regional, not municipal, problems. Utilities serve extensive areas, while mass media bring together people who live over a wide region. People, trade, manufacturing, utilities, and a wide variety of services have all spread outward, making it no longer possible to think of the city and suburbs as separate entities. This recognition of the interdependence of the metropolis is the key to the future of our cities. While policy makers may not be in a position to accept this concept, the urban researcher can underscore the fact of relatedness which in time may result in the emergence of new theories of dealing with the problems of an urban environment.

The problems of one community are relevant to the urban scene as a whole. The scholar's concern with special matters can contribute to the building of an urban tradition and can provide a theoretical basis for a general urban theory and policy upon which the future of our cities must depend.

While beginnings have been made, a massive breakthrough in the field of urban research is still to come. "One urban slingshot or a single urban stone . . . regardless of the hurler or the accuracy of the stone's trajectory" will not fully or finally dispose of the matter.[27] Because the metropolis is complex and its strands interwoven, it defies definition. It has different meanings for different people. A business executive, a wage earner, a shopkeeper, a city planner, a social worker, a member of a minority race, a suburbanite, a "downtowner," a new migrant in the inner core, an elected municipal official—all begin from different premises. Similar goals are not universally shared as to highest priorities. Nor are urban problems always distinguishable from those which society as a whole faces. Not only has our population become predominantly urban, but those areas still rural are increasingly influenced by the spill over of urban culture.[28]

This complexity suggests the advantages to be gained when a group of scholars from a number of disciplines are brought together in their common concern about the urban scene. At the University of Wisconsin, an effort was made to define manageable areas of inquiry for urban scholars. Selected for this purpose were a study of 1) urban dispersal; 2) the processes and problems of policy formation, and 3) urban public finance.

The Joint Center for Urban Studies of the Massachusetts Institute of Technology and Harvard University, when it was established in 1961, concentrated on the structure and growth of cities, urban transportation and technology, urban design, and urban and regional problems of developing countries. A Center for Urban Education created in 1965 in New York City hopes to focus the intellectual potential of higher education on the problems of urban schools. Other interdisciplinary efforts have been initiated at the University of Pennsylvania, Washington University in St. Louis, Rutgers, the University of Pittsburgh, the University of Chicago, the University of California, Northwestern University, Princeton University, and Wayne State University.

Several years ago, Professor Merle Curti acknowledged the national leadership which a group of social scientists had achieved:

. . . they saw that it was important to understand intelligently the profound social and economic changes that were both disturbing and challenging, not only to Wisconsin, but to the whole country. . . . Second, these pioneers worked closely together in an *ad hoc* pragmatic way. They acted as if there were no conflict between the natural and social sciences, as if, in other words, the unity of knowledge was an operative reality. Third, and most telling, these men selected problems for investigation that seemed important or even crucial to the public. . . . It was the positive linkage of social science with faith in a progressive democracy. . . .[29]

There is much wisdom here for the urban scholar who, in selecting the ground on which he intends to stand, perceives the social and economic changes that are challenging the whole country, acts on the assumption that the unity of knowledge is a reality, and selects problems crucial to the public interest.

The university has the further responsibility of making the knowledge its scholars have acquired known in the community and applying it so as to improve urban life. In the past, universities accepted two functions as their legitimate concern—teaching and research. But the extension of knowledge and its application to everyday problems is now an equally legitimate function. The university should not isolate itself but should play a decisive role in advancing democracy. This social utility of education has gained increasing attention, been tolerated in some institutions, and given positive support in others.

The University of Wisconsin was first to give national prominence to this service concept. Its president, Charles Van Hise, contended that it should be an institution for all of the people, active in improving society and in developing a close partnership with the people of the state. It could operate in the market place, he maintained, without jeopardizing its other functions and thereby integrate knowledge with life. It could become the brain of the commonwealth and the laboratory in which popular government could be tested.

There thus emerged the "Wisconsin idea." Charles McCarthy, chief of the Wisconsin Legislative Reference Library, expressed this commitment in this way:

The university has a duty to perform and cannot shirk it. . . . What better way can it pay its obligations than through the production of good citizens and expert help? . . . The writer has found the members of the legislature glad indeed to confer with the expert professor and ask his advice, be it on the question of tuberculosis, the chemistry of gas, or the regulation of monopoly. . . . If the legislature may not secure expert service . . . it will never reach the scientific basis of these great questions now before us which must be solved by the aid of the expert's technical knowledge.[30]

How the results of basic urban research can be rendered understandable and useful to people living in our cities is a legitimate concern of our universities. The benefits of agricultural research have been transmitted to the American farmer during the past hundred years. The cooperative Agricultural Extension Service has reached large numbers of our farm population in every state in the Union, helping to upgrade the quality of life. It has contributed substantially in achieving the dramatic shift from food shortages to substantial surpluses, and in raising the standard of living enjoyed by farm people to among the highest in the world. By gaining support from federal, state, and local sources, and with powerful citizen support, it has established an enviable pattern of service, and demonstrated a clear and unmistakable tie between laboratory findings and their practical application on field and farm.

This is not to say that the methods of the Agricultural Extension Service should be slavishly imitated. Yet there is relevancy in the concept. A Wisconsin newspaper editor described the analogy in this way:

Farmers and farm wives turn to the university to find out about new insecticides, animal drugs, soil helps, grain, poultry, stock improvements, and the answers to barn, home, and design problems. Aren't there wise men on the Hill to devise a service for the poor bedeviled urbanite with his leaky roof, his creaky plumbing, his smelly lakes, patched pantaloons, and short-rationed hamburger? His government needs looking at, too. His streets, his sewage disposal, his traffic, his parking, his bus service, his buying habits could stand a draught of fresh perspective. Not to mention his frayed and outworn notions of his world around him.[31]

Speaking at the opening of the new campus of the University of California at Irvine on June 20, 1964, President Johnson suggested that one of the tasks of the university was to improve the plight of our cities "just as our colleges and universities changed the future of our farms a century ago." "Why not," he asked, "an urban extension service, operated by universities across the country and similar to the Agricultural Extension Service that assists rural areas?"[32] This challenge, that the urban university should do for the people of the city what the land-grant colleges have done in the past century for the nation's population, was earlier issued by Paul Ylvisaker of the Ford Foundation in 1958. He suggested that the Morrill Act of 1862 be rewritten on its one hundredth anniversary for what has now become an urban rather than an agricultural age:

Urbanites, no less than their rural predecessors, need help with family budgets, nutrition, maintenance, land use, housing, vocational guidance, credit, and conservation. And these urban extension services, no less than those provided by agricultural agents, need to be backed with continuous research of the scale and sophistication long ago developed through the agricultural experiment stations.[33]

Title I of the Higher Education Act of 1965, signed by President Johnson on November 8, 1965, now makes it possible for universities to engage in educational programs especially designed for urban and suburban communities.

Yet the analogy of the county agricultural agent must be used with some caution when applied to the urban scene. While the comparison is tempting, it has its hazards. The complexities of city life make diagnosis difficult. The problem of contact and communication between the community and the university is much more involved. Every metropolitan community in America is highly organized. City organizations already existing are performing many extension type services. The university, therefore, does not move into a vacuum when it commits itself to extending services to its urban community. As a result, the distinctive role of the university and that of already existing community agencies is at times ambiguous. For the university to establish an urban extension system, ignoring already existing community agencies, would be unnecessary and unwise.

Urban America also presents a social laboratory entirely different from its rural counterpart. Caution needs to be exercised, therefore, in developing urban agent types. The University of Wisconsin in reassessing its urban extension program concluded that

as we look at the way our urban teams have operated and the direction they now seem likely to take, we see that to some degree the county agent model has led us astray. . . . Social problems seem to rise in geometric progression as people gather in urban places. . . . The governmental system is larger, more intricate, and more pervasive. There is a larger variety of social, religious, cultural, and other voluntary associations. The necessary conclusion with regard to university outreach in an urban area is, therefore, that anything less than involvement of an extensive range of academic interests will be incomplete.[34]

In no area of urban life will the resources and know-how of our universities be taxed more heavily than in dealing with the problems spawned by the people from rural areas who have now settled in the segregated slums of our metropolitan areas. Between 1950 and 1960, for example, New York City lost 1,300,000 middle-class whites. These were replaced by 800,000 underprivileged Negroes and Puerto Ricans. With little preparation for urban life, they live in rapidly deteriorating neighborhoods. Often family histories are characterized by chronic illness, poverty, and separations, while a high percentage of school dropouts and a marked incidence of juvenile delinquency are prevalent. Every city in America has its pockets of poverty characterized by high unemployment, low educational attainment, slum conditions, and disproportionate social welfare demands.

The acute needs of these disadvantaged defy any simple treatment. For these millions, new criteria and techniques are required. Yet universities in the cities have not defined their responsibilities to such problem areas. Many past efforts have been directed toward segments of the population seldom found in the slum areas. Cooperative extension services, for example, were originally designed to reach the farmer, while many general extension activities have had a strong middle-class orientation. For all practical purposes, the lower classes of our urban society have been untouched by the university outreach. Few of their youth attend the university, and only a minute fraction of their adult population has felt its impact.

The problem of the disadvantaged has reached crisis proportions. The impact of university efforts in the much publicized war against poverty has yet to pass the test of relevance and applicability. Many of the traditional methods are not valid; university personnel have yet to learn how to reach the disadvantaged. The university's visibility in the inner core is blurred, while the wide experience of its personnel in dealing with other community problems is often unrealistic in dealing with slum conditions. In these areas the university will find audiences and problems at variance with any that it has encountered. The urban university, therefore, must pioneer with new programs based upon fresh insights and understanding.

The new requirements of an urban society call for innovation and experimentation indigenous to the conditions of urban America. A new kind of "urban agent" will have to be found who can move into the inner core of our cities and give the university a physical presence it does not now have. But the entire university must become involved. A team approach, using the skills of a number of disciplines, holds much more promise than the use of a single agent with only generalized knowledge. For this purpose generalists as well as specialists need to be brought together.

Many of the professionals working in the slum areas are ill prepared to meet the demands placed upon them. Teachers are a case in point. In 1950, only one out of every ten children attending school in our largest cities was disadvantaged. It is now estimated that by 1970, one of every two children in our largest school systems will be in this category. Often from the middle class, and used to dealing primarily with middle-class families, teachers are overwhelmed by slum area children whose values are entirely different from theirs. They need to reorient their philosophy about society. The schools in which they teach will need to adopt fundamental reforms, and add new and special programs. Universities located in cities can play a decisive role in reshaping educational philosophy and practices to meet these requirements. Summer institutes to train teachers of the disadvantaged, now possible under Title XI of the National Defense Education Act, and pre-service programs for future teachers, such as those developed in several of the colleges of the City University of New York, are examples of what can be done in teacher education. Remedial programs in reading, grammar, and mathematics, tutoring programs, the establishment of preschool and nursery centers, and the development of inservice training programs are now all possible as a result of the Economic Opportunity Act.

Throughout much of the nineteenth and early twentieth centuries, our schools had the major responsibility for the Americanization of millions of immigrants. Facilitating this assimilation was one of the major contributions of our school system. An even greater task is now being presented to our schools. It is that of assimilating millions of newcomers who have in the last generation moved into the slum areas of our big cities.

But the problems of the disadvantaged are not the exclusive responsibility of the schools. Slum neighborhoods are characterized not only by inadequate educational opportunities but also by poor housing, low incomes, and high incidence of crime and delinquency. The urban university must develop service and training programs that recognize these realities. Neither the complexity nor the controversial nature of urban life should deter universities in their quest for new techniques and methods. Without duplicating the efforts of community organizations, the university can assist them in a variety of ways, such as helping plan projects, conducting appropriate research, evaluating results, and providing in-service training programs. It should scrupulously avoid duplication of effort, or using its resources in such a manner as to cause existing community organizations to diminish their endeavors.

Creative innovation, rather than performing routine urban services, is the vital role of the university. It should

devote its energies to what might be described as the frontier of urban extension, exploring and testing new ways of relating its intellectual resources to the need of the community for urban knowledge. As it moves into new frontiers it should seek to leave along the way trained persons, institutional arrangements, and habits of mind—especially among urban decision makers at all levels—that will so function as to enable it in good conscience to disengage its resources from established or repetitive operations and reinvest them in exploration. Thus the university can contribute continuously to the strengthening of the urban society and to the maintenance of its own vigor and integrity as a center and source of knowledge.[35]

This innovative role, then, is the central one for the university to play. Since the problems of urban society are multifaceted, the institution's contribution must be selective, qualitative, and special. Projects that can contribute some scientific validity to problems that recur in a number of communities are especially suited to university purposes.

The university engaged in urban extension must constantly ask itself certain questions: How far can its limited resources be extended into the urban field? What activities can be entrusted to other institutions and agencies in the community? What is appropriate for a university to do? What is inappropriate? More than thirty years ago Abraham Flexner, critical about many of the demands being made by society on the university for service, replied that "a university should not be a weather vane, responsive to every variation of popular whim. Universities must at all times give society, not what society wants, but what it needs."[36] The university's involvement in the life of the community, if it is to be effective, must be on its own terms and compatible with its own purposes. Its influence must be on the side of the intellect, with the scholar's point of view paramount. If the university pursues this path, its role can be significant. Here, then, is the special role for the university in the field of urban extension—that of innovator, of commentator, of analyst, of catalytic agent, of critic and advisor.[37]

The university located in the city has the broader task of informing citizens about all aspects of urban America. This is clearly within the tradition of university responsibility. Since education must fit the requirements of the culture in which it operates, a new kind of education designed to help people understand the urban environment is necessary.

For most people living in cities no serious metropolitan problem of crisis proportions, demanding a radical departure from past practices, exists. The average citizen may criticize when the snow is not plowed in front of his home or when his beaches are closed because of pollution. He may complain when he is caught in a traffic jam or cannot find a place to park. But these are minor irritations. He has not yet reached the point of demanding a radical change in the way things are done. Few citizens have, as yet, an area-wide point of view about the problems of the metropolis. The implications of the growing economic interdependence of urban areas are not generally understood, nor is the conflict between that interdependence and the proliferation of political jurisdictions apparent.

An essential ingredient still missing, then, is the concern of the individual citizen. Convinced that he has little opportunity to affect political decisions, the citizen's voice in urban politics is not a dominant one. Here the urban university can furnish leadership. Bringing the policy maker, the civic leader, and the university together can take many forms. At Columbia University, for example, the University Seminar, begun twenty years ago, has attracted hundreds of participants.[38] The underlying theory of the seminar is that knowledge and experience can be synthesized around perennial issues by bringing scholar and practitioner together. The seminar on The City, for instance, has included a professor of engineering economics, a settlement house director, an architect, a police captain, a sociologist, a historian, a school administrator, and a housing official. A bridge of understanding is built that minimizes the separation of different departments within the university, as well as that between the man in the university and the man of affairs.

Another effort to bring the academician into closer association with the policy maker has been a series of seminars sponsored by a group of universities in cooperation with the Brookings Institution. Too often the professional jargon of the scholar has not been understood, nor has his concern with theory been apparent to those who have to deal with specific urban problems. Yet his knowledge is one of the major resources for improving our cities. In such communities as Cincinnati, Baltimore, Memphis, Lansing, and Newark, directors of urban renewal, city planners, mayors and councilmen, representatives of business and industry, and newspaper editors have engaged in dialogue with social scientists from colleges and universities, placing emphasis on the fundamental problems of man in urban society rather than upon any topical issues of the moment.

University programs for urban policy makers can take many forms. A graduate program in public administration offered by the University of Wisconsin-Milwaukee, for example, has had as regularly enrolled students, in addition to a number of department heads and other key metropolitan officials, the two top publicly elected officials in the Milwaukee metropolitan area—the mayor of the city and the county executive. Such high level in-service training is important because many officials

find themselves catapulted, with no particular preparation, into positions of great complexity, and . . . because our whole educational system has somehow failed to come to grips with the problem of educating people for high positions. Add to these considerations the fact that tradition assumes that the mere designation to a high office . . . makes it inappropriate for him to appear in the role of a student, and we have a partial explanation for the frustration of public hopes and aspirations at the point at which they are translated into operative public policy.[39]

The program of urban fellows established at Rutgers University, where key persons are released by their agencies or companies and given financial support to study the urban scene, is an example of what can be done. The careers of those selected for these fellowships have included such diverse fields as social work, banking, education, religion, and journalism. Even agricultural extension has been represented in the program. Since many areas formerly rural have become rapidly urbanized, the urban fellowship program meets a clearly expressed need on the part of agricultural extension workers to broaden their educational background as further preparation for urban life.

Specialized programs for particular groups have been tried by a number of urban universities. Religious leaders need help in understanding the changing character of the urban church. Organized labor is seeking help in expanding member participation in community life. Social workers are overwhelmed by the phenomenon of disintegration. School administrators are dramatically confronted by de facto segregation. Business executives want to understand the economic growth patterns of their communities. In every case, the university has something to contribute if it will communicate with its city and extend its talents and knowledge to those in positions of leadership.

But the university, in addition to reaching the policy makers and civic leaders, should also be in touch with the people generally. An essential component in community betterment is the concern of the private citizen. A high degree of public apathy characterizes the urban scene. Several years ago the voters of metropolitan Cleveland solidly defeated a proposal for a metropolitan county charter. The chamber of commerce, labor, business, both political parties, three daily newspapers, and women's organizations vigorously supported the plan of reorganization. But at voting time, everyone seemed to be for it except the majority of the voters. It was clear that a common ground on which the principals could stand had not been found. In like manner, a study in Dayton, Ohio, revealed that only a minority of the residents of the area had any continuous interest in metropolitan affairs. Less than one quarter of its residents had ever attended a public meeting concerned with a local governmental issue. Only one out of four felt strongly enough on a local issue to try to influence someone else to his point of view.

Urban universities are just beginning to see their opportunities in this important area of community understanding. The Metroplex Assembly, a kind of town meeting via television organized by the Civic Education Center of Washington University in St.

Louis, is illustrative. Linking informal discussion groups around the St. Louis metropolitan area through television, the Assembly has brought ideas and information about the metropolis into the home. Viewing posts, ranging in size from five persons to twenty, have been organized in homes, and television authorities, after presenting facts about a city problem, answer questions or respond to telephoned comments. Forums, lectures, short courses, conferences, preparation of informational materials, assistance in the development of community organizations, radio and television programing can all contribute to a fuller understanding of the problems facing our cities.

In his January 12, 1965, message on education to Congress, President Johnson suggested that the time had come for the university to face the problems of the city as it once faced the problems of the farm. "The role of the university," he declared, "must extend far beyond the ordinary extension type operation. Its research findings and talents must be made available to the community. Faculty must be called upon for consulting activities. Pilot projects, seminars, conferences, TV programs, and task forces drawing on many departments of the university—all should be brought into play."[40] This is indeed a demanding assignment and one that urban universities must accept.

CHAPTER IV

The Urban Campus

HISTORICALLY MOST UNIVERSITY COMMUNITIES HAVE BEEN LO-
cated in physically attractive neighborhoods. With the growth of
cities, however, deterioration of these neighborhoods has taken
place. Since the cost of relocation is prohibitive, many universities
have been forced to remain where they are. As a result, substantial
rebuilding of the neighborhood has become increasingly important. The location of urban institutions frequently makes orderly
growth difficult and physical expansion disproportionately expen-
sive. Hemmed in on all sides, the problem of expansion assumes
mammoth proportions. Many institutions located in the heart of
the city, and often established prior to mushrooming metropolitan
growth, have until recently given little thought to future growth.
San Francisco State College, for example, founded around the
turn of the century as a normal school for the training of elemen-
tary teachers, was originally located in the heart of San Francisco.
No one at the time could have visualized it becoming a major,
multipurpose institution of higher learning with over 15,000 students enrolled, as was the case in the fall of 1964. By 1940 its
five-acre site was bursting with 2,500 students. Nearby church
quarters were rented to take care of classroom pressures, while the
Salvation Army gymnasium was used for physical education classes

and aquatics were taught in the nearby YMCA and YWCA swimming pools. A new site was obviously the only answer, and the move to the present location was completed in 1954.[1]

Other institutions initially located in the outskirts have been engulfed as the irresistible thrust of the metropolis reached outward. For example, a group of educational, charitable, and religious institutions moved to Morningside Heights in New York City at the turn of the century. They were anxious to locate in an attractive open area, yet remain close to the center of the city. But urbanization could not be resisted. The area radically changed in character, with an ensuing steady deterioration of large portions of it. Vigorous measures eventually had to be taken to arrest the process of decay and to provide for an orderly plan of development that would assure a pleasant, healthy, and safe existence for the people living in the area.

The same story has been repeated in many other American cities. Blight, obsolescence, deterioration, overcrowding, and traffic congestion are common in the areas surrounding many urban institutions. These have a stultifying effect on institutional growth and are a deterrent to those wanting to live in the immediate vicinity of the institution. Often the university itself has contributed to these conditions. The need for inexpensive rooms and cheap food and personal services for students has often resulted in the inflow of low cost facilities and services to meet these needs. High population density has led to the conversion of large single family dwellings into rooming houses, "efficiency" apartments, and multiple residences. Zoning violations and sub-standard living conditions have occurred. Traditional street patterns, unable to handle peak load traffic and transportation problems, have impeded the efficient flow of traffic. The absence of adequate off-street parking facilities has aggravated congestion and contributed to hazardous driving conditions. High density land coverage and indiscriminate intermingling of residential and commercial use of properties have resulted in incompatible land uses, while competition for land has often led to undesirable land utilization. Zoning variances and obsolete codes have eroded neighborhood values, and piecemeal measures have not kept pace with the rapidly changing urban scene. Many an urban university today must halt such deterioration and take vigorous steps to help rejuvenate its neighborhood. Thus redevelopment, rehabilitation, conservation, and good urban design have become matters of primary concern to those planning for the future of the urban university.

Some institutions have resolved their dilemma by going elsewhere and making a fresh start. A Report of the Educational Facilities Laboratories describes the experiences of Colby, Goucher, Harpur, and Trinity.[2] Obsolete facilities, noncontiguous property, excessive land costs, and unsavory neighborhoods were factors responsible for the moves. But these institutions were small at the time of their relocation. The largest had no more than 1,300 students. None of them was typical of the multipurpose, complex urban institution.

Some newer institutions have been able to capitalize on the advantages of a fresh start in a new location. The University of South Florida, for example, recently located outside the city limits of Tampa with a campus of over 1,500 acres at its disposal. Opened in 1960, it is situated nine miles northeast of downtown Tampa, a metropolitan area with a population of over a million. With an industrial park south of the campus and a limited access highway system only a short distance away, this new urban university has solved its space problem, even though located in one of America's rapidly expanding metropolitan areas.

Most institutions, however, cannot move. For these it is a fortuitous circumstance that the general flight out of the city shows signs of being reversed. The mass exodus to the suburbs that began after World War II is beginning to lose some of its glamor. The disenchantment that has set in with the promised land of suburbia is also being paralleled by a renaissance that is reaching into the center of many of our major American cities. These efforts to come to grips with aging urban centers are infusing new life into the main stream of the central city. As a result, some blighted and slum areas are in the process of being converted into livable space. Residential and commercial areas, once choice but now suffering from the impact of metropolitanization, are being revitalized.

This metamorphosis should give urban universities renewed hope. Several of them, confronted with the possibility of relocation, have already decided not to move out. Temple University, which surprised Philadelphia a few years ago by buying an 80-acre suburban site, recently reversed its decision, remained in the city, and embarked on a multi-million dollar expansion program. "To retreat from the city," Millard Gladfelter, president of Temple University, declared on its 75th anniversary, "would be to contradict our tradition, our growth, and our potential as a university in an urban setting, and to deny the mood of the times which is a vast population shift to the nation's urban centers."[3] Temple's sister institution, the University of Pennsylvania, in the 1940's considered moving to a 250-acre tract it owned in Valley Forge because of the serious deterioration of its neighborhood. But it, too, decided to remain. The University of Wisconsin-Milwaukee, created in 1956, decided after a lengthy debate, and with a generous offer of a suburban site dangled before it, to remain near the center of the city. The wisdom of this decision was recently reinforced by its acquisition of adjacent institutional properties which more than doubled the acreage of its campus.

There are, of course, practical reasons why many urban institutions are not in a position to move elsewhere and build a new campus. Large investments have been made in existing locations, while the demand for secondhand institutions is limited. But the battle for institutional survival has just begun. As Fred Hechinger has pointed out, "higher education is being urbanized like the rest of American life, and unfortunately this urbanization coincides with the decay of American cities."[4] Testifying in 1959 before the subcommittee on housing of the Committees on Banking and Currency of Congress, representatives of institutions located in urban areas declared that during the next ten to fifteen years, colleges and universities located in urban centers will be called upon to perform an academic miracle. They will be expected to provide educational facilities to far greater numbers of students than ever before in the history of this nation. Physically, they will be required to nearly double their present facilities in order to fulfill their responsibilities. Universities, however, do not have the mobility of industry or the residential builder. Most of these colleges and universities are "landlocked", having no open campus area available for this required expansion. As a practical matter it is virtually impossible for such institutions to assemble usable construction sites through the acquisition of needed land by negotiation.[5]

Consequently each urban university is engaged in a thorough reappraisal of its location, seeking to capitalize on it and to identify itself with those forces that are striving to make the city a pleasant place to live. To be a part of the city and not apart from it is a challenge that urban institutions are beginning to accept, at the very moment when cities are re-examining their place in society and reassessing the means by which they can provide an attractive environment for their people.

These problems of urban location have their parallel in many of Europe's major cities. From early times, Europe's universities have been an integral part of city life. Because of this, a precise identification of university facilities and buildings as distinct from the rest of the city is hard to establish. Since universities have acquired property in many parts of the city and have scattered their faculties over a large area, it is impossible to determine where the university quarter ends and the city begins. The University of London, for example, consists of 33 self-governing schools and a dozen institutes, with its faculties scattered over many parts of the city. In Paris, the University is dispersed throughout the Sorbonne district with additional centers in other parts of metropolitan Paris. Growth by slow accretion over a long period of time and the acquisition of noncontiguous holdings scattered throughout the city are characteristic of many of Europe's urban universities. Yet, in general, they have accommodated themselves to the fact that the university and the city, while bumping and elbowing each other at many points, should maintain an intimate relationship as a condition of survival.

After the war some of Europe's urban universities, in the face of physical destruction and badly overcrowded facilities, gave serious thought to relocation. At the time there was widespread interest in decentralization and diffusion. Heavy congestion and high land costs in the center of the cities where universities were located also created some sentiment to relocate in the outskirts. A second branch of the University of Paris, for example, was established at Orsy, a suburb about 15 miles from the center of the city. Its 160-acre campus, with one of Europe's largest atom smashers and an important research station, was designed to relieve some of the pressure generated by the 80,000 students attending the University of Paris in the congested Sorbonne district. A further expansion of the university at Antony, a suburb of Paris, with cottages for married students as well as other facilities, encourages a further dispersal. Yet there is no agreement that such decentralization is sound. The former vice-president of the National Union of French Students contended that it would create an artificial environment for the student and would isolate him from real life. Students should live in the same neighborhood with the adults they would encounter in daily life, he argued, and should share in the leisure activities of the rest of the population. Only in this way could the student fully capitalize on the educational experience of being in a city with its varied cultural and recreational offerings.[6]

The pressure to remain in the center of the city is strong. The tendency, therefore, is to expand in present locations, to make piecemeal acquisitions of land as it becomes available, and to build high within permissible limits. For example, the Technical University of West Berlin, badly damaged by the war, has remained in its downtown location. Its old buildings are being rebuilt, while new high rise buildings that blend into the surrounding massive skyscrapers, which house West Berlin industry and commerce, are being constructed. The University of Frankfurt, with over 10,000 students on a campus designed for 2,000, is planning many multi-story buildings and intends to move its medical and natural science faculties to another part of the city. It reached this decision because of the expense of land acquisition, and also because the university has full and final responsibility for the relocation of all dispossessed families. The University of Paris, in spite of its suburban campuses, is building new and high in the Sorbonne district. Facilities for science faculties have recently been built on stilts over archaic and antiquated buildings in order not to incur the wrath of the venerable wine merchants of the Halle Aux Vins district.

Occasionally a university on the Continent has an opportunity to start from scratch, unhampered by a city that envelops it on all sides. The Free University of Berlin and the new university to be built in Bremen are examples. But these are exceptions. Most of Europe's universities have historically been located in cities. Their roots are so deeply planted, tradition so strong and investment in physical plant so substantial that relocation is seldom seriously considered. Europeans build for centuries, and the prospect of abandoning facilities, old though they are, is not a happy one for them. Even total destruction during the war is not sufficient incentive for these institutions to begin anew elsewhere.

The pattern of development for British universities has been markedly different. Oxford and Cambridge, of course, followed the collegiate pattern of spacious setting and architectural magnificence, with student and teacher living under one roof. In the nineteenth century, however, civic universities such as Manchester and Birmingham were founded in large cities. From their inception they existed to meet local needs and were supported by local benefactors. The existence of a large student body living at home and working in the neighborhood while attending the university was of primary importance in determining their location.

In more recent times, with generous financial grants either by the Ministry of Education or by local educational authorities, students have sought entrance to universities outside their home areas. This increase in student mobility has minimized the need for establishing new universities in densely populated areas, and has resulted in the development of national rather than local or urban institutions. Since the war seven new universities have been granted charters, bringing to 30 the number in the British Isles. These institutions have not been located in the major cities. Thus, universities have been authorized for Brighton, with a population of 156,000; Canterbury, with 28,000; Colchester, with 57,000; Coventry, with 260,000; Lancaster, with 48,000; Norwich, with 121,000; York, with 105,000.

That a university is being planned for Coventry, even though a major university already exists at Birmingham, ten miles away, is of special interest. Birmingham, which began as a local university primarily to meet the needs of its immediate area, has lost much of its provincial character and has gained national and even international stature in some of its areas of specialization. Two-thirds of its students, and half of those attending the University of Manchester, come from beyond 30 miles, while the proportion of students living at home has fallen markedly in recent years.[7] Further expansion of British universities is contemplated as a result of the 1963 report of the Robbins Committee. Applying the principle of enlarged educational opportunity to the university level, it concluded that there should be a place in higher education for all who can satisfy entrance requirements and who wish to continue their education. Its target calls for an expansion in places for higher education from the present 216,000 to 560,000 by 1980–1981, with intermediate targets of 328,000 places in 1967–1968 and 392,000 in 1973–1974. To accomplish these goals the Robbins Committee recommended the creation of six additional universities, the upgrading of ten technological colleges, the creation of five special technological colleges comparable to the Massachusetts Institute of Technology, and the conversion into universities of ten other existing higher institutions.[8]

There are a variety of reasons for the decision to locate new British universities in communities that some might describe as quiet country towns, isolated from the hubbub of metropolitan life.

In addition to increased student mobility, a controlling factor has been the size of site available for a new campus. Two hundred acres is considered minimum so that all university activities, including residence halls and playing fields, can be integrated into a single complex. This factor, of course, rules out the possibility of new institutions being located in the center of cities. Both the excessive cost of land and the lack of availability of contiguous property make such a location impractical. There are some who have concluded that the decision to locate new institutions far from the center of the cities reflects a desire to retreat into the past. Professor Harry Ree of the University of York suggests that "nothing could be further from the truth, and if it had been true, the new students themselves would have seen to it that such a retreat would be halted and reversed." There were good and simple reasons why those localities were chosen, he suggests, for "in these towns, for the most part, it is possible to acquire land, not only for immediate building, but for later expansion, at a far lower cost than in the big cities where most of our universities now are. This has meant that the new universities can be planned, each as an organic unit, on a campus, instead of sprawling over a large city."[9]

For those urban universities in America that have decided to remain in or near the center of the city, there can be no further delay in the development of plans for future expansion carried out in close working relationship with the neighborhood in which the institution is located. The character of the area has important consequences for the institution. The need for good living conditions for faculty and staff, for instance, is urgent, and a determined effort must be made to keep them close to the campus. As Julian Levi points out, a university "must be a community of scholars, not a collection of scholarly commuters. The cross-fertilization of many disciplines and fields, so essential to productive research and teaching, is possible only when a university community exists as a place of residence."[10]

Scholars need to be near libraries, laboratories, and offices on a continuous basis if they are to perform the academic duties required of them. Many medical and hospital activities and advanced research programs require around the clock supervision. Comfortable living close to the campus must be provided so that faculty can put the facilities of the institution to maximum utilization. Without a congenial atmosphere near the campus, faculty and staff will leave it when their specific duties have been performed. As a result the faculty member is "part neither of a university nor of an urban community, nor do circumstances encourage him to fulfill his duties in the educational enterprise."[11]

But the area around the university must be attractive and safe for still another reason. Many of the activities generated by the university are of great interest to the people of the community. An attractive environment, therefore, will encourage non-university people to move into the area to continue their education, to find constructive avenues for their leisure, and to enjoy association with academic people. This intermingling of town and gown is important, too, to university personnel, for it gives them an opportunity to share common interests.

The creation of a university community which relates itself to the surrounding neighborhood and becomes an organic part of it must become a major objective for urban universities. Chancellor Hutchins of the University of Chicago quite properly pointed out in 1950 that

a university can consider itself fortunate if its members live in the same neighborhood and have frequent social contacts; if it has an architectural plan that brings the members of the faculty into easy professional association and an academic organization that requires them all, however occasionally and superficially, to consider together the affairs of the university or any other problem outside their specialties. The importance of these items should not be underestimated; for, to take one example, the influence on speculative and practical studies of having the professional schools at a distance, frequently at a great distance, from the universities of which they are nominally a part has been uniformly bad. . . . A university should be an intellectual community in which specialists, discoverers, and experimenters, in addition to their obligation to their specialties, recognize an obligation to talk with and understand one another.[12]

Important to university personnel is location in a neighborhood that provides the amenities necessary not only for their own comfort, safety and convenience, but also for their families. Good schools, parks, adequate police protection, close proximity to other cultural institutions, and rapid and efficient transportation will attract and hold a faculty. It is especially important that good schools be available, since faculty members want their children properly prepared for college. Central to the creation of the West Philadelphia Corporation, for example, has been its participation in improvement of the public schools. According to its executive vice-president, Leo Molinaro, schools are the magnet that draws and holds a community of families, and only with good schools will faculty and staff want to live and raise families in the area.[13] While academic people have an affinity for urban living, urban universities are often at a disadvantage because they cannot provide the amenities which faculty and staff require. An urban university can no longer disregard these factors in developing and building its staff. When Chancellor Hutchins stated in 1945 that his university had "the unfortunate distinction of having the worst-housed faculty in the United States," he highlighted a problem characteristic of many institutions located in blighted and deteriorating areas.

One of the earliest and most dramatic efforts to cope with the corroding effect of metropolitan growth occurred in the Hyde Park-Kenwood area in which the University of Chicago is located.[14] An irrevocable decision had been made early in its history that it should remain an urban institution. By 1951 its campus comprised 100 acres and represented an investment of more than $200 million. As a result of a heavy influx of low income whites and Negroes, a steady deterioration occurred that alarmed not only university officials but other citizens of the area. The South East Chicago Commission was created in 1952 to solidify university and neighborhood opinion. State legislation made it possible for neighborhood corporations to organize and, by acquiring 60 per cent of the property in any given area, obtain eminent domain rights over the remaining 40 per cent. Subsequently with the support of the city, state, and federal governments a project of major significance emerged. As a result, "major surgery" has been performed in the Hyde Park-Kenwood renewal area, comprising about 900 acres and involving an anticipated expenditure of almost $200 million in university, local, and federal funds. Dr. Kimpton, in announcing his resignation on March 29, 1960, as chancellor of the University of Chicago, was able to report that "in common with other urban universities, the University of Chicago was confronted with the problem of encroaching blight. If the university was to exist, that threat had to be removed. It has been removed, and we now have assurance of a stable community in which the university will have the environment essential to its life and activities."[15]

Chicago proved to be a test case of what can be done in the battle against urban blight. The program has not been without severe critics. The university's support of restrictive covenants, until they were declared legally unenforceable, coupled with the strong feeling of many Negroes in the area that university expansion was directed against them, resulted in considerable hostility against the university. Its concentration on moving the power structure of municipal government, rather than first achieving agreement with the neighborhood, and its neglect of public information and education further impeded progress. Yet its advocates point with pride to a substantial curtailment in the crime rate, an increase in the median income of families in the area, and the fact that 85 per cent of the faculty and staff of the university now live within walking distance of the campus. Julian Levi, a major figure in this development, concluded that "our experience is that urban renewal is like lifting a watermelon. It's not hard once you get your arms around it."[16]

The Chicago example was followed by other urban universities.

At the initiation of Chancellor Kimpton the presidents of Harvard University, Columbia University, the University of Pennsylvania, Yale, and the Massachusetts Institute of Technology met in New York City on April 12, 1957, to exchange views and share common experiences. As a result, the Association of American Universities undertook a nationwide study to determine what could be done to prevent further deterioration of neighborhoods adjacent to urban universities. The survey, published October 13, 1958, under the title *Study of Neighborhood Problems of Urban Universities,* included fourteen universities ranging in size from 8.34 acres to 983.4 acres. Limited acreage for future expansion and tremendous expenditures anticipated for future land acquisitions characterized each campus. Seven of the fourteen institutions had five acres or less available for expansion, four institutions had less than fifteen acres, while only one had more than forty acres for future growth. These institutions expected to spend $150 million for land acquisition during the next six years, ranging in square foot cost from a low of $1.59 to a high of $25.

One of the most important efforts to recognize the problems facing urban universities was the amendment passed in 1959 to the Housing Act of 1949, known as Section 112. Its stated purpose was to establish a cohesive neighborhood environment compatible with the functions and needs of institutions of higher learning. Some institutions had already taken advantage of urban renewal prior to the passage of Section 112, but the result had not been impressive. The 51 per cent residential requirement of the Housing Act was particularly restrictive to universities. Under this provision, 51 per cent of the area to be cleared or of the proposed new use had to be residential in order to be eligible for urban renewal. Yet what universities needed were not residential but campus facilities, while much of the area that surrounded the university was not residential, but commercial and business.

There were other reasons, too, why universities had found urban renewal, prior to the passage of Section 112, a mechanism not suited to their purposes. Owners of residential and commercial property adjacent to the university often resented what they considered encroachments on their rights. City officials, constantly looking for ways to broaden the tax base of the city, expressed alarm over properties being acquired by a university for educational use, only to be taken off the tax rolls. A study completed in Boston and reported in the *Wall Street Journal* warned that the city would not be able to provide the necessary services to its citizens if the uncontrolled expansion of tax-exempt institutions was permitted to continue.[17] Since land which universities acquired for their educational purposes was tax-exempt, they were thus not in a strong position to gain city support in their behalf for renewal projects, or to convince the city that such land acquisitions best served the city's interests.

However, Section 112 of the Housing Act gave urban institutions a strong bargaining position. Non-cash credits accumulated by them could now be used as the city's share of the cost of renewal projects. This could be done without departing from the original concepts of the Housing Act of 1949. This act had provided for a program of federal loans and capital grants to cities for the purpose of acquiring and clearing land in blighted and slum areas, for preparing it for redevelopment and then disposing of it at a fair re-use value in accordance with an approved urban renewal plan. Since the price to be paid for cleared land was usually less than the cost of acquiring, clearing, and developing it, the means for writing off the differential in cost was provided through federal and local grants. As a general rule, the federal government, through cash capital grants, bore two-thirds of the write-off costs, and the locality, through local grants in aid, bore the remaining third.

Since local public agencies were required to contribute one-third of the net cost of an urban renewal project, the incentive for locating such projects in university interest areas was frequently missing, especially if, upon acquisition of renewal property by the university, it would become tax-exempt. But Section 112 of the Housing Act changed all this. The university's cost of acquiring land in the open market, the expenditures incurred in connection with the clearing of such land, and the cost of relocating tenants could now be used as credits toward the city's share of renewal projects. As a result, an attractive inducement for cities to launch redevelopment projects in or near college and university areas was created. A number of cities were quick to grasp the advantages of using expenditures made by a university for physical expansion as bookkeeping credits which the city in turn could use as a share of its contribution to a renewal project. If, for example, over a five-year period a university had expended $500,000 on improvements, and an urban renewal site adjacent to it was then selected, the city could apply the $500,000 expended by the university as a credit to help meet the city's share of the redevelopment cost.

As a further incentive Section 112 permitted credits accumulated in excess of the city's share of the net project cost to be applied to urban renewal projects undertaken elsewhere in the city. Other benefits to the city resulting from such an arrangement became increasingly evident. As sections of the city were cleared near urban institutions, new residential and commercial development often opened up. Such redeveloped areas provided a substantial increase in property tax income, even though large portions of the renewal area were designated for university or college purposes.

The urban institution now had at its disposal a method by which it could acquire land otherwise not available to it except through eminent domain. The difficult problem of the "holdout" was resolved, with the result that land could be acquired in large blocks. This in turn made it possible to plan for campus expansion in a more orderly and realistic manner. A recent expenditure by one of New York City's urban universities of $3,300,000 for 7.5 acres in an urban renewal area on Manhattan's west side, for example, would not have been possible if the area had been purchased parcel by parcel from individual owners.

A means now existed by which the institution could purchase land at a considerably lower cost than in the open market. James

Kelso of the Massachusetts Institute of Technology estimated, for example, that in Boston, institutions would have to spend $10 to $15 a square foot for land purchased in the open market, while the cost to the institution would be no more than one-fifth of this when the purchase was from the city through an urban renewal project. Purchasing in the open market could spell financial disaster for some urban institutions. But with the purchase price of re-developed land computed on the basis of the value of the cleared land, rather than its original value, urban institutions could now purchase additional land at a reasonable cost and at fair re-use value.

Within five years after the passage of the amendment, over 75 institutions had already taken advantage of this urban renewal mechanism. The fact that most of these applications are of recent origin underscores the importance of Section 112 in creating a method helpful to both the institution and the city. Scores of institutions are now finding it possible to expand existing campuses or, as in the case of the campus in Chicago of the University of Illinois, to create entirely new ones. Victimized by an unfavorable environment resulting from blight and deterioration, and hemmed in on all sides by land uses not congenial to a university community, more and more institutions are taking advantage of the opportunity provided by the special provisions of Section 112 of the Housing Act.

But a university located in an urban area must set its own house in order and create a campus environment conducive to its purpose —that of learning and discovery. Its campus development plan should be so designed as to support and enhance its teaching, research, and public service functions. Its concept must encompass the total environment of learning which includes, in addition to classrooms, libraries, and laboratories, many other institutional facilities. Residential quarters for faculty and students and for other professional and middle management people, special research facilities, and provisions for sororities and fraternities, as well as coordination with the surrounding commercial facilities, parks, and schools, must all be considered.

To accomplish this objective, universities must think in terms of a new urban form related to the general environment of which they are a part. A campus in the Jeffersonian tradition, with large open spaces, elm-lined malls, and ivy-clad buildings, has little relevancy in most urban situations. The acreage needed to develop an urban campus is not nearly as great as is generally believed, while the provisions of the Housing Act of 1959 make it possible for private as well as public institutions located in deteriorating urban areas to acquire land at considerable write-down cost. Yet urban universities have not faced up to the possibilities of relating their plans to the requirements of the urban scene. The advantages of compactness resulting from an urban location have not been fully grasped. Ground areas can be expanded indefinitely by use of the high rise and multilevel principles. Limited acreage need not result in a cramped, circumscribed condition. It is possible to build facilities that are within easy walking distance of each other and that use intervening spaces for open plazas, student gathering places, and as visual relief to provide a proper architectural setting for buildings and structures.

The new campus of the University of Illinois in Chicago, located at Congress Circle, is designed to create such a compact urban campus and to serve the city in which it is located. Provision is being made to accommodate an eventual enrollment of 20,000 students. It is located at a point where three expressways converge, and is close enough to the center of the city so that students can take advantage of its rich cultural resources. In its academic core of 40 acres, provision is being made for a campus that avoids both the sprawling open areas of many residential colleges and the canyon type institution devoid of charm or beauty.

Costs of land acquisition are too high and the resources of the institution too limited to permit lavish use of land. Expanded graduate offerings and demand for other specialized programs, research parks in close proximity to the university, the need for housing students and faculty, all require the most careful use of land. But the automobile poses one of the most serious problems. Dependence on the automobile is a much more acute problem in an urban university than it is in the typical residential college or university. In urban universities where there are a number of local students (sometimes as high as 90 per cent of the total student body) and a large number of commuting part-time students, the problem of the automobile is critical. As the public service functions of the university expand, and as people come to the campus for seminars, workshops, institutes, and to use research laboratories, hospitals, and other facilities, the problem is compounded. More often than not, urban universities are surrounded by commercial and residential properties which permit little room for expansion of off-street parking facilities.

A study at Big Ten universities and the University of Chicago concluded that an additional 20,000 parking spaces in surface parking lots would require an additional 140 acres.[18] A university parking committee at the University of Washington recommended that provision be made for 15,000 parking spaces by 1970. The problem of providing adequate parking thus assumes major proportions. In many communities, pressure is mounting to force universities to restrict the use of student automobiles. But those charged with university traffic and parking have been reluctant to impose necessary controls. The automobile should not be allowed to run unbridled through the campus, disrupting pedestrian traffic and interfering with the academic purposes of the institution. Many institutions have tried to minimize or even eliminate street parking within the campus. Yet to force the automobile into the neighboring areas creates new problems. Neighbors are always displeased over university automobiles parked in front of their homes. The acquisition of additional land on the edge of the campus is often prohibitive in cost. A study at Drexel Institute in Philadelphia concluded that when the cost of land approaches $5 a square foot, multistory parking facilities become less costly than surface facilities. Circumstances, of course, differ from campus to campus. This is a problem that must be dealt with as a part of the total plan for the campus and the neighborhood.

The urban university is, of course, intimately related to other institutions in the area. Its neighborhood and its inter-institutional relationships, therefore, require constant attention. The people who live and work in the area need to understand its problems, its goals, and its necessity to expand. The urban institution must be aware of the doubts and apprehensions of its neighbors about an expansion that is inevitable but not fully understood. Urban Renewal Commissioner William Slayton reported that "in assisting urban renewal projects in the immediate vicinity of universities, we have frequently observed that there exists an almost universal attitude in non-university people of hostility toward the university and its authorities."[19] The institution must declare the geographic limits of its future expansion, assist in developing a sound plan for the neighborhood, and make known to its neighbors its intentions in an understandable manner. Specifically, appropriate areas need to be designated for residential and commercial development, professional establishments, fraternities and sororities, religious foundations, housing, and other auxiliary activities.

The university and the neighborhood must plan about their common problems together so that conflicts can be minimized and varying interests reconciled. This was in the minds of those who, in 1962, organized the University Hill Corporation in Syracuse, New York. Representing Syracuse University, the State University of New York, and merchants and property owners in the area, the bylaws of the corporation listed these among its purposes: to encourage long-term planning; to provide a vehicle for consultation with the city as it develops its community renewal program; and to provide a mechanism for reconciling all interests of the neighborhood so that urban renewal would not be stalled.

The desire to preserve a predominantly residential area in the face of an expanding urban university led to the establishment in 1960 of the Lakeside Community Council in Milwaukee. Here was a neighborhood that had completed virtually all of its building before World War II. Yet the census of 1960 reported over 90 per cent of the structures in sound condition. As late as the 1930's, one-third of the families listed in the Milwaukee Social Register were living in this area.

But in the postwar years the character of the neighborhood had begun to change, highlighted in 1956 by the establishment of the University of Wisconsin-Milwaukee, which by 1965 had almost 13,000 students and plans to double its enrollment in the next ten years. The Lakeside Community Council was then founded not only to study the problems generated by the expanding university but also to enlist support in solving them and helping preserve the residential character of the area. Recognizing that the area is still one of the best residential sections of the city and that a university is an asset to a city, the Council has set about to deal with problems of parking, traffic and transportation, education, housing, planning, and general community improvement. Serving as a transmission belt between the university and the community, the Council seeks to minimize conflict and to dissipate confusion and anxiety resulting from lack of communication.

Urban universities attract to their area a host of institutions: foundations, libraries, hospitals, national associations, religious and charitable organizations. Morningside Heights in New York City is the home of a score of institutions including Columbia University, Union Theological Seminary, Teachers College, Riverside Church, and the Jewish Theological Seminary. Close to the University of Chicago are a wide assortment of institutions including George Williams College, the Museum of Science and Industry, the headquarters of the American Bar Association, and the International City Managers' Association. Wayne State University is in the heart of Detroit's cultural center which includes the Detroit Library, the Detroit Institute of Arts, the Children's Museum, the Detroit Technical Museum, the International Institute, and the Rackham Memorial Building.

Faced with similar problems and often in competition for the same land, these institutions have found common cause and have combined their resources in the hope of dealing more effectively with their situation. One of the first efforts to coordinate the requirements of a cluster of institutions occurred in Cleveland. Prompted by common concerns, nine institutions in 1957 created the University Circle Development Foundation. Today it has 29 members, including institutions of higher learning, hospitals, churches, museums of art and natural history, and the symphony orchestra, as well as other charitable and social service institutions. Located in an area that covers 500 acres, its staff and student populations exceed 18,000 persons. Its twenty-year master plan calls for an expenditure of $175 million for buildings, land acquisition, parking facilities, recreational areas, road construction, and housing.

Particularly significant has been the willingness of members to relinquish to the Foundation some of their institutional sovereignty. Each member has yielded its power to acquire land and has agreed not to negotiate separately with any governmental body for special favors or dispensations. The Foundation sells land to the institutions as they need it, and exercises architectural review over each institution's plan, to be certain that it follows the pattern of development laid down in the master plan. The Foundation has its own police force, its own shuttle bus service, and parking facilities within the Circle, and generally assumes responsibility for the overall development of the area. Viewing its role as one of coordinating the efforts of a number of institutions to help in the task of rehabilitating a large portion of Cleveland's east side, Neil Carothers, president of the Foundation, recently reported that "the diligent pursuit of realistic goals by a group of cooperating cultural institutions is more than a match for the forces that today are threatening the existence of the urban cultural center in America."[20]

Other notable efforts to achieve institutional and neighborhood cooperation have come into being. Morningside Heights, Inc., was formed in New York City in 1947 to restore an area that was rapidly deteriorating. At one time this had been one of the most desirable locations in the city, encompassing Riverside and Morningside Parks. But obsolescence, deterioration, overcrowding, inadequate community facilities, and congestion have occurred in recent years. Over an area of approximately 500 acres, 57 per cent of the residential buildings had been built before the turn of the century, and less than 3 per cent in the last 30 years. Notwithstanding, real estate prices had been skyrocketing. While in 1950 property in the area could be acquired for 95 per cent of its assessed value, by 1958 the average purchase price exceeded the assessed value by 25 per cent.

To halt deterioration and to make provision for needed institutional expansion were the aims of Morningside Heights, Inc., an organization of twelve educational, religious, and medical institutions. Among its goals are: a program of decongestion, including redevelopment, code enforcement, and good urban design; clearance of badly deteriorated and obsolete buildings, with provision for new residential development; improvement of the over-all physical appearance, taking advantage of the famous educational, cultural, and religious buildings in the area; improvement of circulation, through separation of vehicular and pedestrian traffic and modification of the street system; provision for additional off-street parking; improvement of the educational and recreational facilities of the area; and realization through redevelopment and neighborhood improvement of a better balanced tax base.[21] Critics have heaped blame on the corporation for its slow progress and its lack of concern for the area. But it has to its credit some achievements including the development of several major housing projects and the approval of a general neighborhood renewal plan for the area.

The West Philadelphia Corporation, organized in 1959 by five educational and medical institutions, is located in a 370-block area across the river from the downtown Philadelphia business district. This area too had been going downhill. Families were leaving. Transients were moving in. Many residential and commercial properties were deteriorated and decayed. Yet the area had some attractive homes and the most impressive concentration of educational and medical institutions in the city of Philadelphia, with more than 12,000 employees and an annual payroll of $47 million. Eager to assure a favorable environment in which people could live and work, the West Philadelphia Corporation was created to establish "a true community of scholars within the larger urban community." It hopes to achieve this objective through a concerted, large-scale program of renovation of existing properties, by planning of school programs to make the area inviting to families with children, by coordination of the long range expansion plans of the institutions of the area, through redevelopment of a substantial portion of the area, and by the creation of an industrial research park. Of particular significance in the development of this project has been the active participation of citizens.

Often, people in the neighborhood of a university are hostile to its expansion either because it displaces existing commercial and residential development or because it removes property from the tax base. The principle that institutions which use their property for educational purposes should be exempt from taxation is well established. Judge William Hamersley, Connecticut jurist, once described it as "public policy too clear to be questioned." He elaborated his position in this way:

The principle that property necessary for the operation of state and municipal governments, and buildings occupied for those essential supports of government, public education and public worship, ought not to be the subject of taxation, has been with us accepted as axiomatic. It has been incorporated into the constitutions of several states. It has been inseparably interwoven with the structure of our government and the habits and convictions of our people, since 1638. . . . It stands squarely on state interest. To subject all such property to taxation would tend rather to diminish than increase the amount of taxable property. Other conditions being equal, the happiness, prosperity, and wealth of a community may well be measured by the amount of property wisely devoted to the common good in public buildings, parks, highways, and buildings occupied as colleges, schoolhouses, and churches. To tax such property would tend to destroy the life which produces a constant increase of taxable property as well as some benefits more valuable.[22]

Cities are more than compensated for any tax losses by the benefits they receive in income, employment, cultural and educational advantages, and other special services which the university provides. For one thing, faculty and staff employment is a substantial asset to a city's development. With its 5,000 employees, Yale University, for example, is the second largest employer in New Haven, surpassing both the New York, New Haven and Hartford Railroad and the Southern New England Telephone Company. The payroll for its 3,000 non-academic employees amounted to nearly $11 million in 1960–1961. Its orders for services, supplies, and equipment totaled $8 million, while building permits issued to the university accounted for 51 per cent of the total issued by the city.[23]

The University of Cincinnati has reported an annual payroll of $9 million and supply and equipment purchases of another $1.5 million, with expenditures for research grants involving several millions. Non-resident students, in addition to tuition and fees, spent $4–5 million, while parents and visitors from out of town, attending athletic events and professional conventions and meetings brought by the university, accounted annually for 80,000 visitor days at $20 a day.[24] The University of Pittsburgh reports that payroll taxes increased by a larger amount than the property tax losses resulting from land acquisitions; the university was next to the largest private employer in the city, and in six years had spent over $100 million on capital expansion; an anticipated disposable income by 1970 after taxes, insurance, and savings of well over $100,000 a day.[25]

Higher education is one of the most important growth industries in the United States today. At least $15 billion will be spent in the next ten years for building programs. Much of this will be spent on the campuses and surrounding neighborhoods of urban institutions. $250,000,000 will be spent in the Oakland district of Pittsburgh to create a research park, and to meet the capital requirements of the institutions of higher learning in the area. $175,000,000 is to be spent in the next twenty years in the University Circle area of Cleveland. Institutions in the Morningside Heights area of New York City have already spent $80 million and have plans for new buildings within the next few years for an additional $64 million. In the ten-year period ending in 1962, institutions of higher learning in the West Philadelphia area had spent over $70 million, and they contemplate spending another $117 million on capital improvements in the five-year period ending in 1968. Programs of equal magnitude are being projected for the Hyde Park-Kenwood area in which the University of Chicago is located.

The benefits of an expanding university to an urban area are evident in other ways also. Many efforts are presently under way to revitalize cities by attracting research-oriented industry. Engineering and scientific endeavors draw millions of dollars of research and development contracts into the area, while university research attracts industry, especially if it depends heavily on research and new technology. Private research laboratories also gravitate toward universities and technical institutes, since they are prime sources of scientific data, have rich library resources, and provide graduate training for scientists and engineers as well as other personnel. Hence the clustering of research laboratories and growth industries around such great centers of learning as Harvard University and the Massachusetts Institute of Technology.

John Fischer points out that newer growth industries differ from the more traditional ones in that they produce items of small size but great value. They do not use huge tonnages of raw material and fuel, hence do not have to locate near ore bodies or coal mines. They usually operate their plants without noise, smoke, or smell, and are in situations where the quality of the product, rather than wage costs, is decisive. Their one critical requirement, he concludes, is brain power, which they must attract to keep ahead of competition. This they can do best by providing a pleasant environment for their personnel to live in and by locating near great universities, for

scientists can easily be persuaded to move to an area which has a complex of good universities. There they can keep in touch with the research under way in the best laboratories. They can consult whenever necessary with the leading minds in their fields. Above all, they have company. In the evenings they can visit with friends who share their interests and talk their language. And not merely with other scientists.

These people frequently are true intellectuals, with a wide range of interests. They like to live in a community of scholars—historians, writers, sociologists, and even an occasional artist—and they enjoy being near good libraries, good orchestras, good art galleries.[26]

Many urban universities are already capitalizing on such assets with industrial parks beginning to spring up in their shadows. In Philadelphia, a University City Science Center, consisting of a science research institute, a complex of industrial research laboratories, and a conference center, located adjacent to the University of Pennsylvania, Drexel Institute, and other institutions, has now come into being and will provide an unusual urban environment for scientific activity. In Cleveland, a University Circle Research Center is in the making, cooperating with private industry in developing research installations nearby. In Pittsburgh, a research park in the Oakland district two miles east of the city's business center is in the planning stage. To be located in a ravine between Carnegie Institute of Technology and the University of Pittsburgh, it contemplates a $250 million complex utilizing outstanding institutions of higher learning and a wide assortment of scientific and cultural institutions to achieve its goal.

The educational and cultural complex which emerges when institutions find common cause can materially alter the character of urban America if developed in a number of our metropolitan areas. For such an urban center in addition to becoming an important symbol for the city of the future, can become a major intellectual and cultural core for the entire metropolitan area it serves. Here, as the University Circle in Cleveland envisages it, can be created "a physical entity in which people enjoy the city. It can fulfill a function similar to the cathedral squares of medieval times or the village greens of eighteenth century New England. Such an area can provide essential experiences which are impossible to achieve in the helter-skelter, formless development of contemporary cities."[27]

The university should, therefore, take imaginative steps to expand in the area where it first took root, and assist in the renewal of its neighborhood. But whatever measures it undertakes, it must have the full understanding and support of its neighborhood. Much of the hostility to the university has resulted from the university's long standing indifference to the problems of the area. In addition, conflicts have often arisen between its own needs and the desires of the people of the neighborhood. To avoid becoming involved in a tangle of community hostility, the university must realize that it cannot exist apart from its city or remain detached from its neighborhood. Only through an identification with the city of which it is a part can the dual good of needed expansion for the university and renewal of the neighborhood be achieved.

>\< CHAPTER V

The Urban University Student

MORE THAN HALF OF THE STUDENTS ENROLLED IN AMERICAN colleges and universities today are living at home while attending college.[1] Their number will continue to rise. Since ours is an urban society, more of our youth will be brought up in cities, will be educated there, and after completing their education will remain there to work and live. A study in Wisconsin in 1961 found that the heavily populated, high income areas of southeastern Wisconsin provided a higher rate of college attendance than any other region in the state. It showed that counties with high income per capita, close to a number of institutions of higher learning, and *with a large urban population*, were also the counties with a high percentage of high school graduates attending college.[2]

The steady migration from farm to urban communities suggests that most future undergraduates will be commuters. This mobility of our population will be an important influence in the future development of our universities, and must be reckoned with.[3] Peter Drucker has suggested that within a generation, resident campuses will have become obsolete except for graduate and professional education. The trend of living away from home while attending college, which was the standard pattern a generation ago, is certain to be reversed as costs of attending college continue to climb and as larger numbers of young people from the lower income classes go to college. The urban university holds a special appeal to the student who lives in the city, needs to work on a part-time basis, and wants to attend an institution of higher learning. Even prestige institutions located in big cities report a surprisingly large number of their undergraduates coming from the immediate vicinity. For others, the trend is more marked. In New York City, there is the long standing tradition of the tuition-free municipal college. Dr. Thomas Evans Coulton reported, for example, that at Brooklyn College all students were residents of New York City; nine-tenths of them had never lived outside the city, and half had never traveled beyond its immediate environs.[4]

A larger percentage of the student body of an urban university live at home than of its nonurban counterpart. Wayne State University is typical. Its recruitment of undergraduate students has been predominantly local. In 1960, 98 per cent of them were residents of Michigan, a great majority coming from nearby Wayne, Oakland and Macomb counties. Almost 80 percent of the unmarried undergraduates were living with their parents. Three-fourths either were working or hoped to be employed sometime during the academic year. One out of eight full-time undergraduates and three out of five part-time undergraduates were married, making for an over-all undergraduate average of one in three.

During the first semester of the academic year 1964–1965, the University of Wisconsin's urban campus in Milwaukee had 78.2 per cent of its undergraduate student body coming from Milwaukee County. In contrast, 80.2 per cent of the undergraduates on the Madison campus came from outside the county in which it is located. Of the undergraduates in Milwaukee, 28.3 per cent were married, compared to 7.6 per cent for the Madison campus, while 28.2 per cent of its undergraduates were 21 years and over, compared to 23 per cent for Madison. Students attending urban universities are older on the average, and more of them are married. They are also more likely to be holding jobs—either full- or part-time—while attending the university.

Historically we have been committed to the residential college and to leaving home while attending college, and have judged it a heavy handicap to be a student commuter. Yet the concept of the commuting student is an old one. Traditionally the European university has been urban. On the Continent students live either with their parents or in lodgings scattered throughout the city. The spacious setting, the architectural magnificence, and the community life at Oxford and Cambridge are not characteristic of Europe's more urban institutions. The collegiate way, with students and teachers living together, is not possible for the large numbers now enrolled in the urban universities of Europe.

Some, indeed, contend that such exposure is not necessary. Writing about the University of London at the beginning of the century, Sidney Webb contended that the high degree of affluence and the social privilege on which the old university rested were not and never could be provided by London conditions, and even if they could, students might hesitate to take advantage of them. To study in order to be able to engage in leisurely pursuits is, in fact, contrary to the bias of many of Europe's university students who have no financial security, can enter the university only with substantial financial subsidy, and must earn their living in a competitive world as soon as their university work is finished.

For the commuting student attending Europe's urban universities there is, however, stimulation and variety of many kinds. "In loco parentis," in which the university assumes parental functions, as is often done here, is alien to the European university. Not only does the student have more freedom of choice in the selection of his courses and in class attendance, but his interests are broader and more urbane. While organized extracurricular activities as they are known in this country do not exist, there is a wide assortment of student political clubs and organized religious groups in many European universities. National organizations of university students play an important role in the development of opinion on matters of public policy. Fee increases and failure to provide adequate educational facilities have often been the occasion for student protests. Demonstrations, for example, against French policy in Algeria or British policy in Cyprus reflect the students' deep concern about questions of national policy, while in West Berlin, students at the Technical University specializing in engineering constructed a tunnel under the Berlin Wall to assist refugees in escaping from the East. Students have organized to secure health benefits, more generous financial aid programs, and special considerations for access to the city's cultural and recreational opportunities. Understanding of public issues and a sense of responsibility about the world around him are an important part of a student's educational exposure.

But the city itself holds many attractions for the European university student. Henry Commager points out that when Americans go abroad for study or teaching, they do not seek out the universities in the smaller towns. Rather

they head for the big cities. And this is because they know that they can count on an exciting relationship between university and community in almost every country of the Old World. What lures the American student is the life of the boulevards, the cafes, the bistros; it is the Latin Quarter, it is the opera and the ballet, the theater and the experimental film; it is the bookshop on every corner, the dozens of newspapers in every city; it is the mature student body, educating itself, joining in the risks of life, taking an active part in literature, journalism, art, and politics. It is, too, the beauty of the cities that they know they can count on—not just the beauty stored away in museums, but the beauty of houses that have been allowed to grow old, of parks and squares instead of parking lots, of riverbanks not given over to industry but to pleasure, of gardens in the heart of town, of bridges that you can walk across without risk of life, of bicycle paths that parallel busy boulevards, of sidewalk cafes, and of carnivals on street corners.[5]

If this is true of the American student who goes abroad, it is equally true of his European counterpart, who finds the atmosphere of the city with its pulsating life congenial. For most European students who attend universities in large cities, there is a noticeable absence of organized social life on campus. Students are considered a part of the city, where they find their recreation and stimulation whether in the libraries and bookstalls or in the bistros and beer cellars. Thus, while Europe's urban universities may lack the gracious living and congenial atmosphere of the American residential college, the environment of the city affords the urban university student varied opportunities that are full of excitement and stimulation.

There are innumerable advantages of the city to the student, but there are also certain limitations. The transition from high school to college for an urban university student is much more gradual than for those who are leaving home for the first time to attend college at a distance. Hence change for the urban student is not nearly as marked, and the transition somewhat easier. This fact often makes it difficult for the student to accept an image of the university that sets it apart from his earlier education. Urban universities have not succeeded in establishing in their students an understanding of those unusual characteristics of a university that distinguish it from their high school experiences.

The commuting student is often slow to break away from high school habits and the more rigid discipline to which he has been accustomed. Some students, who doubt their ability to do college work and need to make only a small initial investment, enter an urban university on a trial basis without a strong personal commitment. Hence the stimulation of a new educational experience, with its unlimited intellectual opportunities and its endless exposure to new knowledge, tends to escape them. As a result they do not always bring an adult attitude toward learning, but fall back upon the practices to which they were accustomed while attending secondary school.

The home and the parent are important influences in the life of the commuting student. Television, financial problems, family responsibilities, and competition with siblings were all identified as being of considerable importance in a study of entering freshmen at Brooklyn College.[6] Many parents hover protectively over their children and continue to influence them to a much greater degree than is true of the student who goes away to college. The unmarried commuting student, because he lives at home, is inclined to accept family and neighborhood values. Even though he may rebel and resent the pressures of the home, he is less likely to throw off the restraints of the past or to be as venturesome as his counterpart who has left home to attend college.[7] The married student, on the other hand, has non-university obligations that directly affect his education. On many urban university campuses from a fourth to a third of the undergraduate student body are married. Need to support a family and other responsibilities to wife and children condition a student's outlook about many university extracurricular activities.

The need to work while attending college often prevents the urban student from taking full advantage of university campus life. He finds his loyalties divided, his outlook restricted by his former associates, and his activities controlled by influences unrelated to university life. Often he attends the university for part of the day, works to earn his way for another part of the day, and then returns to his home for the remainder of the time. His daily routine is interrupted and compartmentalized, and many influences conducive to a good climate for learning are dissipated. His opportunity for social expression is often limited and he is denied exposure to a wide variety of campus activities. Many campus influences beyond the courses which the student takes, such as peer relationships, responsibility-taking experiences in university affairs, and out-of-classroom contact with faculty, are vital to the development of a university student. But the commuter, "half at school and half at home," unable to take full advantage of these opportunities, is inclined to view his education narrowly, concluding that attendance at classes and the completion of assignments for them fully meet his educational requirements.

The fact that large numbers of urban students work while attending the university also causes them to be job-oriented to their course of study and disproportionately interested in the practical benefits of a university education. The fact that urban universities themselves often have a vocational or professional emphasis in their educational program tends to overstress this aspect of the education of the urban student. The disproportionate number of students enrolled in engineering, commerce, nursing, and pharmacy is a case in point. One urban university in a large Midwestern city, for example, recently reported this distribution of its undergraduate enrollment: letters and science, 1,371; engineering, 1,591; education, 1,219; business administration, 1,259; nursing and health, 294; applied arts, 754; home economics, 192; pharmacy, 251. Enrollments in professional courses were four times those in letters and science.

Family background obviously conditions the attitude toward a university education. A generation or two ago it was the exception for a student of working-class background to enter college. Today, the number of college students from working-class homes exceeds that from upper and upper middle class homes.[8] Because his financial resources are limited, the parent in a low income bracket is not always in a position to assist his child in going to college. A recent survey showed that low income parents who wanted their children to go to college had done little to make this a possibility by specifically saving money for it. Because of income limitation such parents were more "present oriented" than "future oriented."[9]

Many urban university students, therefore, are job-oriented throughout their university education. Ordway Tead warned that

our students have to be made to realize that they are not in college solely to get what they can in terms of self, in terms of economic advancement, and in terms of a grave psychological separation from the background out of which they have come. The college fails fatally if it does not help its graduates to realize that they are there to discover the directions in which the claims of truth and beauty and righteousness lie, and to become committed to those above and beyond the claims of a purely personal career.[10]

There are, then, limiting factors that influence the life of an urban university student. But there are also many compensations.

The city itself is the greatest asset available to the urban university student. In "The Case for the Asphalt Campus," David Boroff reported proudly on the transfer to his own New York University of 1,500 undergraduates from campuses in all parts of the country. Many had became disenchanted with the isolated residential campus and were lured to the urban university by the excitement of the metropolis. "The city, in effect, is the student's campus— asphalt instead of greensward, the subway instead of the convertible, and real life instead of nursery games."[11]

In the past the city university has been considered as a place where students went who could not afford to go elsewhere, or where parents continued to supervise their children in a way not possible if the children left home to attend college. The College of Charleston, America's first municipal college, was established to afford "to all classes of our citizens an opportunity for their children to receive a classical education, and yet to be under parental control."[12] The antipathy to cities as sites for colleges was so pronounced early in our history that the charter of the University of North Carolina stipulated that it was not to be located within five miles of any seat of government or law court. "In Georgia the trustees succeeded in getting as deep into the woods and as far away from civilization as possible; in 1801 they selected a hilltop in northwest Georgia, acquired a tract of forest, and called it Athens," while Tusculum College in Tennessee boasted that its pastoral location guarded it "from all the ensnarling and demoralizing influences of a town."[13]

But this has now changed. With all of its ugliness and disenchantment, the city still is an important generator of civilization and culture. A suitable substitute for the spirit that makes it has not yet been found.

What is this spirit? . . . The spirit of the city arises from its social heterogeneity. The city may also be culturally, even racially, heterogeneous, a place where different languages are spoken, different customs practiced, different gods worshiped. Always it is a brilliantly exciting contrast of the monotony of a village in which life is bound to the cycle of the seasons. The city has the heady excitement of politics with its periodic crises and occasional pomp, its whispering campaigns, conspiracies and rumors, its public press and factionalist parties, with its essential mystery of power. The city has color and variety in its markets, bazaars, and workshops. It has the glittering bubble of entertainment; circuses, games, dancing-girls, music, theaters, restaurants, taverns. . . . The city thus becomes a place of immense cultural vitality, where the consciousness of self is brought to an acute sensibility. Ideas are formed, change in fads and fashions is the order of the day. News and the discussion of news are essential to it. Here the present and the future intersect. The true urbanite is always *au courant.* There is a place for scholars who peer into the past and into cosmic space. Every major creative effort either originates or comes to full bloom in the city. Here the important decisions are made.[14]

Dr. James Hester, president of New York University, contends that the urban university "encourages engagement with the realities of life." Aside from its many cultural advantages, the city provides the urban university student with the finest laboratory for his studies. The courts, hospitals and clinics, social centers, manufacturing plants, schools, industrial and research laboratories, offer the future engineer, lawyer, physician, nurse, social worker, and teacher unlimited opportunity for professional development. It was not accidental that many of the state universities founded in the nineteenth century in a rural setting established professional schools such as medicine, pharmacy, nursing, dentistry, and social work away from their campuses and in the large population centers of their states.

Many urban universities have developed cooperative work-study programs to bring the urban student in touch with the realities of city life. In 1906, the University of Cincinnati pioneered with the cooperative system of technological education, combining theoretical knowledge with firsthand experience.[15] Starting with 27 students and 13 firms, the university recently reported that more than 3,300 undergraduate co-op students were placed in more than 600 companies throughout the United States.[16]

Today over 60 institutions conduct cooperative programs. At

Northeastern University in Boston, for example, engineering firms, manufacturing companies, public utilities, government agencies, banks, railroads, insurance companies, wholesaling and retailing outlets, hospitals, social agencies, publishers, advertising agencies, libraries, schools, and development and research organizations all employ university cooperative students. Although cooperative education programs predominate in such fields as engineering and business education, they can be applied advantageously in other fields as well.[17]

A Study of Cooperative Education in the United States under the chairmanship of Dr. Ralph Tyler concluded in 1960 that

The academic potential of cooperative students is equal to that of non-cooperative students. . . . The cooperative experience provides meaningful opportunities for the student to see the relevance of theory to practical situations and affords him opportunities to practice making applications. . . . Cooperative education makes a positive contribution to society by attracting able young people to college who might otherwise never consider continuing their education beyond the high school. . . . Business and industry are enthusiastic about cooperative education. . . . Because of the financial remuneration received by students for their cooperative work, the cooperative plan makes higher education feasible for many talented youth who might otherwise find college prohibitive. Contrary to frequent criticism of cooperative education, students are able and do enter into the life of the college as effectively as non-cooperative students. . . . The five years of college required by most cooperative programs is viewed by more than 85 per cent of students and graduates as no handicap in getting started in a career. . . . The necessity of shifting attention from classwork during campus periods to jobs during the work periods and back is not a serious educational problem. . . . the cooperative plan makes possible the more effective utilization of college facilities. . . . the vast majority of cooperative students and graduates felt that their original hopes and expectations for selecting cooperative education were realized.[18]

But the city also has much to offer the urban student in pursuit of understanding his total environment. Students today are intent upon being activists and socially useful. The Peace Corps, the

Northern Student Movement, and recent efforts in the South are ready proof that many of today's university students are committed and eager to serve society. Off-campus experiences for learning are abundant in every metropolitan area. The city provides a laboratory where students can enrich their whole college experience. But the urban student, often a commuter, may move from one part of the city to the other—from home, to university, to place of work, and home again—without being aware of either its problems or its opportunities.

An effort must therefore be made to take greater advantage of the opportunities for service in the city. Opportunities for volunteer work, for example, are many. The university student can tutor disadvantaged youth. College undergraduates, training to become teachers, can help harassed teachers in the inner core by serving as assistants. In this manner they can gain an understanding of what it means to teach in city schools. Students preparing for social work, nursing, public health, business and commerce can perform many constructive tasks in the poverty areas.

The opportunity for involvement in community action is unlimited. Yet it has seldom been viewed as a means of broadening the urban student's outlook. Living at home while attending the university can be limiting, especially where the student finds little help in the home to achieve an understanding of his problems. To widen his horizons and to expose him to some of the more critical problems of our society needs the attention of those charged with the development of the urban university.

The lack of a large number of resident students on campus at many urban universities results in a somewhat different response to student participation in matters of broad social policy. In contrast to the European student, where an activist role is accepted as commonplace, the urban student on American campuses disengages himself from many of the major social questions of the day. The Los Angeles and Berkeley campuses of the University of California and the Milwaukee and Madison campuses of the University of Wisconsin offer striking contrasts in the degree of involvement by students in such matters as civil rights, international policy, and academic freedom.

The student living at home is often on campus only for his regularly scheduled classes, while the continuation of parental authority discourages a more independent and assertive attitude on his part. The married student, on the other hand, is preoccupied with family responsibilities and job needs, and therefore finds little time or inclination to engage actively in the arena of politics and social policy. Thus there is an absence of the kind of social ferment to be found on resident campuses, where the tradition of freedom and participation is long and honorable and where a sense of cohesion and community not possible on an urban campus exists.

The image of the urban university as one that caters primarily to students who live at home to save money needs correction. Many urban universities have already begun to broaden the geographic base of their student body by encouraging a core of resident students to attend. The presence on campus of non-commuting students, representing diverse nationalities and many geographic regions, exposes the local student to some of the more cosmopolitan elements of society. Some urban universities are now taking steps to house on campus a portion of their student body from beyond the immediate environs of the city in which the institution is located. Residence halls, a rarity on most urban campuses a generation ago, are becoming commonplace. The University of Pittsburgh, for example, had virtually no students living on campus ten years ago. By 1970 plans call for 5,000 to 6,000 resident students. The University of Pennsylvania has stated that by 1970 every undergraduate should be housed in a unit either owned or supervised by the university. The University of Wisconsin-Milwaukee has initiated a residence hall program that will house 20 per cent of its expected 25,000 students ten years hence.

Urban universities have an unusual opportunity in the development of such residence hall programs. Since many of them have had no housing, they can experiment in relating study space to

living quarters, classrooms to dormitories, and using residence
halls for out-of-classroom experiences. Opportunity should be provided the commuting student to live on campus in university residence halls for periods of a semester or longer. Shorter stays should
also be encouraged. If it is appropriate to plan off-campus trips for
the resident student, is it not equally valid to make provision for
short stays on campus for the commuting student? The use of the
residence hall as a meeting place where the commuting student
can discourse with his fellow students, with members of the faculty,
and with neighbors and townspeople provides an opportunity for
him to be kept on campus and to share in out-of-classroom activities. Over a century ago Cardinal Newman identified the importance of such communication in these words:

When a multitude of young men, keen, open-hearted, sympathetic, and
observant, as young men are, come together and freely mix with each
other, they are sure to learn one from another, even if there be no one
to teach them; the conversation of all is a series of lectures to each, and
they gain for themselves new ideas and views, fresh matter of thought,
and distinct principles for judging and acting, day by day.[19]

Other out-of-classroom campus experiences should be made
available to the urban university student. The Union has great
potential educational value. It need not be only a service agency
providing food, books, supplies, and recreational facilities. Dining
rooms are important, but so are informal meeting rooms, art
galleries, music rooms, special libraries, and theaters. While traditional recreational facilities are proper, so are painting and
sculpting studios, browsing rooms, photographic laboratories, and
hobby shops. A Union that is only an entertainment center and a
supply depot is narrowly restrictive and inadequate.

In its program the Union should support the educational purposes of the institution. The educational and cultural fare should
augment what is already available in the city. President Harold Case
of Boston University highlighted the importance to his own institution of a Union facility in these words:

As an urban university is set in the midst of distracting influences of noise, speed, complexity—so there is added need for a unifying force. One such influence is the Union building. Designed to invite broad outlook, joining massive areas with intimate retreats and enjoyable recreation with serious study, releasing the forces to join the common interests of students in the midst of the varieties of objectives, the Union provides a friendly, happy atmosphere for human association, with kinship and unity of purpose the by-products.[20]

The university bookstore, too, can play a vital role in the life of the urban student. Henry Commager contends it should even be maintained at a loss just as is the case with the theater, music, and athletics. Asserting that it is as essential to a university community as the library and the laboratory, and a good deal more important than the stadium, he concludes that "we have only to reflect on what Blackwell's and Parker's mean to Oxford, what Heffners and Bowes mean to Cambridge, what Thin's and Grant's mean to Edinburgh, what the scores of bookshops on the Left Bank, or in the university quarters of London or Copenhagen or Utrecht, mean to these communities, to realize what we are missing.[21]

When Congress passed the National Defense Education Act in 1958 it declared that "the security of the nation requires the fullest development of the mental resources and technical skills of its young men and women. . . . We must increase our efforts to identify and educate more of the talent of our nation." This should be a major concern of all our colleges. But the urban university has a special obligation to relate itself centrally to breaking down barriers to education, for the pool of untapped talent is greatest in our cities while the costs of education for a student living at home can be kept to a minimum.

A tremendous social revolution has been taking place in American higher education in recent years. Approximately 20 per cent of the children of the upper working class are enrolled in colleges and universities today.[22] A study in Wisconsin showed that 20 per cent of the children of service and semi-skilled factory workers planned to attend college. This study concluded that

pending more definite knowledge than is now possessed about human promise, the wise course is to provide abundant opportunity for outstanding human ability to rise at any stage in the educational process. This procedure seems wasteful, but if a gold miner finds it profitable to process one ton of ore to secure a half ounce of gold, it seems that human ability should be considered no less precious. The open door policy squares with the fundamental American belief about the worth of the individual in our society and with the aim that each shall have the opportunity to educate himself to the limit of his capabilities.[23]

The opportunity for children of low income families to pursue their education at home is all the more critical in view of the fact that expanded scholarship assistance by select private universities and liberal arts colleges has not always attracted substantial numbers of lower economic level youth to them. Elmer West has reported on a study of 65 institutions where the number of students receiving aid coming from families with an income in excess of $11,000 was four and a half times as large as the number from families with less than $3,000.[24] In a similar vein Robert Havighurst reported that the fathers of those awarded scholarships by the National Merit Scholarship Corporation were predominantly engaged in middle-class types of work, while Harvard's National Scholarships were given mainly to sons of middle-class families. He concluded that the publicly supported urban university kept the financial barrier for a large proportion of students down and thus made higher education available to many young people who wanted it.[25]

To seek out and provide financial assistance for qualified students from low income families requires a coordinated effort by the institution. A total assessment of the financial requirements of a student to permit him to continue his education is necessary. Loans, scholarships, student employment, and now work-study programs should all be viewed as part of an over-all, coordinated effort to bring to college many who would otherwise not come at all as well as to encourage those who are already enrolled. Relatively few institutions have such comprehensive financial aid programs. Yet they are an indispensable part of the effort of every university that has committed itself to expanded educational opportunity. Many qualified students with limited means and living in our big cities can especially benefit through such coordinated efforts.

As recently as ten years ago few institutions had comprehensive loan programs. Today, such programs are considered an indispensable part of a student financial aid program. Similarly, part-time employment as an integrated part of a student financial aid program has not yet been universally accepted. Nor have the full advantages of a work-study program been realized. "Assignment of student jobs is rarely related to students' financial needs or to the judicious balancing of work with other forms of financial aid to provide the total financial support necessary," was the observation of the Advisory Committee on National Student Financial Aid Programs of the College Scholarship Service. The committee concluded that "the serious need to bring more young people into college often goes unrelieved for lack of planned use of guaranteed jobs to reduce the formidable barriers that, in one way or another, keep many young people out of college."[26]

Such work-study programs are especially suitable for many high school graduates who could profitably continue their education in urban universities, but do not do so. Some students, with weak college motivation, are discouraged from going on, especially if their parents are unwilling to commit substantial funds for this purpose. Such youth, not always eligible for scholarship assistance and with little parental encouragement, often do not continue their education. By expanded student employment programs, needy students for whom a university education is beyond their financial means and for whom a loan program is not a satisfactory solution can continue an education that would otherwise be denied them. Since federal funds are now available for youth of low income families, universities should set aside additional funds for work-study programs for students who do not qualify under the federal program but who can benefit from part-time employment. Such programs can encourage institutions to find new ways of using students in existing jobs and can create new employment opportunities that have substantial educational value for the student. The possibility of uncovering jobs related to a student's course of study or to his professional or vocational goals has not been fully explored by most institutions.

Increasing costs of education and the selective admissions policies of many institutions, which often act as a deterrent to minority groups, give the university located in the city, with its large disadvantaged populations, a special opportunity. Sixty per cent of the Negro families in the United States have incomes of less than $4,000 annually. The reluctance of many institutions to admit Negroes because of greater academic deficiencies and weak prior schooling is a matter that needs prompt attention.[27]

The "smothering of talent" that has resulted from failure to extend full opportunity to this group has caused a substantial loss of creative and skilled manpower, the result of "the cumulative impact of poverty and ignorance at home, degraded neighborhoods, poor educational facilities, limited job opportunities, and the ever-present fear of rebuff."[28] Negroes, Puerto Ricans, and other racial and ethnic minorities have a much smaller proportion of their people enrolled in colleges and universities than the total national college age group. While Negroes, for example, are one-tenth of the population, they contribute only one-twentieth of the nation's college enrollments. Of these over 80 per cent are enrolled in segregated colleges. Less than 2 per cent of the northern undergraduate student body is Negro. A large part of this group is enrolled in low tuition urban institutions, yet even here the ratio is only a fraction of the city-wide ratio of Negro to white.

This lack of opportunity is all the more serious because there is evidence that youth from culturally disadvantaged families often make a better record in university work than their high school performance or their college aptitude tests indicate they are capable of making. Richard Plaut's studies suggest that the identification of talent involves more than the measurement of academic aptitude and achievement.

For pupils who come from homes of low socio-economic status, the attitudes, interests and motivation have a subtle but important cumulative effect on scholastic aptitude and scholastic achievement. . . . Pupils who have spent their lives in homes usually of low socio-economic status are deprived of the opportunities for stimulation of academic interests and attitudes, except in rare instances. Such pupils have been deprived of the motivation of books, magazines, newspapers, and cultural and academic occupational experiences of parents. For such children, the usual tests of academic aptitude and achievement may underestimate their potential ability.[29]

There is, then, need for a thorough talent search that is not limited to those groups that are either culturally advantaged or are free from the financial burdens attendant on college going. If it is to be the goal of our society to allow each person to develop to the limit of his ability, then "closing the doors of educational opportunity to any young person because of race, creed, origin, or sex is manifestly intolerable under the democratic principles upon which the United States is founded." It was in this context that the President's Committee on Education Beyond the High School urged every American, "as a matter of high moral obligation, to work toward the abolition of such barriers wherever they exist."[30]

The urban university is uniquely situated to relate itself to the promise of American democracy that all should be given opportunity commensurate with ability. To deal realistically with this search for talent it is necessary to face up to facts about disadvantaged youth that do not apply to other segments of our society.[31] Family environment among Negroes is often disruptive. As a result, an understanding of the structure and functioning of the Negro family is imperative. Individual motivation also needs to be understood. The Negro youth's knowledge about job opportuni-

ties is often restricted; hence, his ambition to continue his education is drastically limited. Since no culture-free tests have been
devised, the Negro's performance on such tests is not a good guide
to future potential. The record of students participating in the
National Scholarship Service and Fund for Negro Students suggests that the disadvantaged are likely to do better in their college
work than their aptitude tests indicated they would.

Any program that seeks to uncover talent among our disadvantaged youth requires a concerted attack on all conditions that now
stand in the way of development. To deal effectively with this
problem requires a multifaceted approach

including the structure and functioning of the Negro family and community and the values and behavior of both Negroes and whites, as
well as the present state of and future prospects for his educational and
economic opportunities. Each facet is inseparably connected with all of
the others. A deficiency in any one area will react adversely on all other
areas, just as improvement in any area will lead to cumulative benefits.[32]

This assumes an early identification of talent, counseling and information programs aimed at encouraging promising youth to continue their schooling, contact with parents, many of whom will
not have had the educational opportunities being sought for their
children, an understanding attitude by community agencies that
deal with teen-age youth, and the full cooperation of the schools
where the academic preparation for college takes place.

Recognizing the importance of this matter, the University of
Wisconsin announced a program to encourage those who have
academic talent to aim at a profession and to continue their education. Financed by university funds and by foundation grants,
Project Destiny was begun in 1964 in cooperation with the Milwaukee public schools. More than 40 per cent of those graduating
from its high schools continue with some sort of education. Yet in
the schools where the disadvantaged predominate, the percentage
is less than 10. In a predominantly Negro school in Milwaukee,
for example, fewer than 50 students entered the University of

Wisconsin-Milwaukee in a three-year period even though more than 600 had graduated.

To make college available to more of these disadvantaged youth, Project Destiny seeks to identify capable students, gives to selected persons individual attention while in high school, works closely with the parents, provides remedial services and supplementary programs of enrichment, and makes available financial assistance for fees, tuition, books and out of pocket expense. By this means it hopes to attract students capable of doing college work who, for a variety of reasons, have not found their way there. Research growing out of the project should also assist in a better understanding of present methods of selecting, advising, and encouraging students from underprivileged families, who have manifested capacities for doing college work.

Other urban universities have also developed programs aimed at this special group.[33] The City University of New York has initiated a program of admissions for hundreds of students from "pockets of poverty" in New York who may not have grades ordinarily required for admission but who show strong motivation and special qualities of leadership and creativity. UCLA has a program that combines part-time jobs, loans, grants in aid, and scholarships to qualified students who are economically and environmentally disadvantaged. In St. Louis, special institutes for disadvantaged high school students with college potential have been begun. A number of institutions, through Educational Services, Inc., have established pre-college centers offering remedial instruction in mathematics and English. They are also developing special testing materials to lessen the academic disadvantages of the student and to minimize the remedial burdens often placed upon the college.

The university located in the city, in close touch with the schools and other community agencies, and having direct and continuous access to the student as well as the parent, should be challenged to bring to realization the American commitment that all should be educated to the limit of their capabilities regardless of their station in society. The explosive character of technological change and the increasing complexity of our social organization also require that we give greater attention to the vast reservoir of human abilities and skills needed to meet a variety of shortages that demand advanced training. For there is

the constant pressure of our ever more complex society against the total creative capacity of its people. . . . Society as a whole must come to the aid of the individual—finding ways to identify him as a unique person and to place him alongside his fellow men in ways that will not inhibit or destroy his individuality. . . . By its attitude toward the creative person, a free society can actively insure its own constant invigoration.[34]

✕ CHAPTER VI

The Urban University and the Arts

THE URBAN UNIVERSITY CAN DO MUCH TO SUPPORT ART AND culture. Not only is there now wider participation in cultural pursuits, but the arts have come to play an increasingly important role in the life of our society. This commitment to the arts is of recent origin. In *Democracy in America*, Alexis de Tocqueville expressed concern about the possibility of the arts ever really flourishing in America. In few civilized nations, he wrote, had great artists, distinguished poets, and celebrated writers been as rare as in the United States. This, he contended, was the inevitable result of our belief in equality which tended to divert men from concepts of beauty to other goals. Love of physical gratification, the excitement of competition, and the charm of anticipated success turned attention away from the pleasures of the imagination and the labors of the intellect, and were so prevalent that it was difficult for Americans to deviate, even momentarily, from this emphasis.[1]

There was considerable truth in de Tocqueville's contention. Considered as something mysterious and forbidding, the arts through much of our history were relegated to a minor position. As a result, the view emerged that the pursuit of a native culture was not a legitimate goal for us to seek. Some argued that the arts were synonymous with affluence and monarchy, and their importation to America would be out of harmony with the new spirit of republicanism.

But cultural activities today are assuming increasing importance. There is greater participation. Also it is more sophisticated. There is considerable evidence that we are moving toward a more creative period. Consumer spending on the arts, as reported by Arnold Mitchell of the Stanford Research Institute, rose twice as fast between 1953 and 1960 as spending on all recreation, and six times as fast as outlays for spectator sports or admissions to movies. Over 50 million Americans participate today in amateur art activities, as players of musical instruments, as art photographers, as Sunday painters, sketchers and sculptors, as community theater performers. Mitchell reported that there are today more piano players than fishermen, as many painters as hunters, twice as many who attend concerts and recitals as those who see major league baseball games, and more theatergoers than boaters, skiers, golfers, and skin divers combined.[2]

Many reasons for this burst of interest in the arts can be cited. Technical advances have made it possible for tools, books, records, cameras, and other materials to be bought at modest cost, thus giving to millions of people access to cultural outlets formerly denied them. Increased leisure has provided a broader and more sympathetic audience. More people have more goods and more leisure at less cost. But the factor contributing most to the cultural explosion of our times has been the upward thrust in educational attainment. As more people have moved up the educational ladder, with professional, technical, and managerial personnel increasing more rapidly than others, support for the arts and cultural activities has shown a marked upswing. Universities and colleges have helped produce a clientele that sustains a climate in which the arts can flourish. Whether such audiences are discriminating enough to upgrade substantially the quality of cultural life is perhaps debatable. Whether urban universities have grasped the opportunity to develop imaginative quality programs in the arts is also open to question.

Yet there is a strong tradition to support the university that seeks to enlarge its efforts in the arts. James Perkins, president of Cornell University, in opening a series on the university and the arts in cooperation with the Lincoln Center for the Performing Arts, pointed out that it has been traditional for universities to accept new responsibilities as society has identified new areas, and that the willingness of the university to adapt itself to a changing society has resulted in its becoming one of the great social inventions of all time. The encouragement and support by it of the arts, he suggested, is in keeping with both the purposes of society and those of the university.[3] In like manner, the Rockefeller Panel in assessing the place of the university in the performing arts concluded that it is "one of the natural homes for the arts and should be encouraged to extend the range of its hospitality in the years to come."[4]

While the performing and creative arts have been included only recently in the university curriculum, and still have not been enthusiastically embraced by many, the history and criticism of the arts is generally accepted as a proper area of study. Courses in theory, history, philosophy, and interpretation have long been accepted as legitimate offerings in our universities. More recently, courses in appreciation have been added. The establishment of schools of fine arts is gaining support, especially in newer universities. Such efforts to bring together all the arts seek to overcome a tradition, still prevalent in many older institutions, in which architecture is lodged in engineering, dance in physical education, theater in speech, and creative writing in English. When a School of Fine Arts was created at the University of Wisconsin-Milwaukee in 1963, for example, it was the clear intention of the university to create an administrative structure that would make it possible to see the arts in their natural relationship to one another. As a result, courses in the arts and mankind, and the theory and criticism of the arts, are required of all students enrolled in a school which includes art, music, theater, and the dance.

But whatever the organization may be, we are obliged, after

examining the total range of possibilities, to turn to the university for major support of the arts. Not only is it a suitable instrument for this purpose, but it is one of the few institutions that can give the arts a secure and stable base. The Committee on Policies of the Association of Graduate Schools recently declared that

since the nineteenth century, a steady migration to the campus has occurred of types of instruction that formerly took place largely in independent schools and institutes. . . . Training in the creative arts has joined this procession. Academic institutions now increasingly perform functions that formerly fell chiefly to independent drama schools, art institutes, music conservatories, and other forms of personal instruction not associated with educational institutions of more general purpose. [And] modern universities seem increasingly to be expected to offer instruction in the creative arts beyond the bachelor's degree.[5]

Some of the skepticism about the propriety of programing for the arts has now disappeared, with the compatibility of the arts and academic life gaining increasing recognition. The artist as scholar and craftsman has had to earn his way into university circles just as the experimental scientist did earlier. The Report of the Committee on Visual Arts at Harvard University (1956) reflected this new orientation toward a more sympathetic acceptance of the arts in the modern university:

The present status of the arts within most universities is as though instruction in science were confined to the history and philosophy, and involved neither scientists nor scientific laboratories. Less than one hundred years ago this seemed to many altogether right; now it would be conceded by all to be absurd.[6]

The report concluded that the great artist is great both as an artist and as an intellectual.

Such a view has not yet been generally accepted. The training of performing artists has not received unreserved endorsement. Yet there is no reason why the university cannot become a center for the performing arts, or why a thoroughly professional environment outside the university should provide the only satisfactory avenue for training the professional artist. The Theater Group at the University of California-Los Angeles and the University of Michigan Professional Theater Program offer interesting examples of organic affiliation between the professional and the university. The influence of the former extends beyond the campus into the wider metropolitan area, while the latter, in demanding high professional achievement, contributes to the improvement of taste. Such university-professional affiliations also result in a new focus for the arts on campus. At the University of Michigan, for example, internships, playwrights in residence, and lectures and seminars conducted by outstanding professionals add substantially to the more traditional theater programs on most university campuses.

If the university is to assume major responsibility in the training of the professional artist, it will require some major adjustments. Speaking before the Association of Graduate Schools at New Orleans in 1961, W. McNeil Lowry of the Ford Foundation suggested the need for a radical change in attitude on the part of the university toward the aspiring professional studying at the university, as well as for an opportunity for professional apprenticeship removed from the academic environment.[7] On the latter point, the arrangement between the University of Minnesota and the Tyrone Guthrie Theater, in which graduate students work in the professional theater, is a good example of an unusual relationship made possible by the virtue of a university located in a major city having a professional theater. The American Conservatory Theater in Pittsburgh, a cooperative effort of Carnegie Tech and the Pittsburgh Playhouse, represents a new approach to combining training and performing, by bringing together the seasoned professional, postgraduates from drama schools, and students at Carnegie Tech interested in the theater as a career. The charge is often made that the university does not understand the special kind of concentration required for the training of the professional performer and is not prepared to make the necessary adjustments to meet his requirements. An arrangement in which the aspiring artist can have some of each—the environment and discipline of the stage as well as an academic exposure—is possible where the university and the cultural agencies of the city work out cooperative arrangements.

The university that commits itself to the performing and creative arts as a major area of endeavor will need to re-examine many of its assumptions and practices. Innovations and new concepts of training must be sought. It will be necessary to revise existing curriculums in the creative arts, to reverse traditional procedures for evaluating achievement as they affect faculty rank and promotion, and to establish new criteria for determining admission of students, giving an individual's creative work and potential high priority, as well as to provide the professional, who has achieved recognition because of the excellence of his work, a rightful place in the university community.

The university in the city has a special opportunity to support programs in the performing and creative arts. Large centers of population maximize diverse opportunities and provide an important setting in which the university and the artist can carry on their efforts. In the same manner that a small community can provide adequate hospital facilities but cannot support a system of advanced medical research, can support a movie house but not a foreign language cinema, can maintain a library for its people but not a major research facility with rich and varied book collections, so it cannot have a major museum, art gallery, symphony orchestra, professional theater, or opera. "The big metropolis can make all the greater joys possible. That is because it presents the statistical probability that within the boundaries there are enough potential customers for each experience which may be caviar to the general."[8]

But the city provides not only the clientele so necessary for the support of the university's efforts, especially if it sees its role as that of innovator and experimenter. It also provides an abundance of materials and a setting important for the artist to carry on his creative activities. He needs the stimulation of the city, the opportunity to capitalize on a variety of audiences as well as to mingle with other artists and to have a place to harbor his non-conformity. But the artist also needs time for study and contemplation, facilities where his works can be seen and heard, and economic security so that he can concentrate on his creative effort. The artist in residence at a university located in the city thus can have some of both worlds—that of the university which provides him economic security, freedom to engage in his creative activities, and the stimulation of students, and that of the city with its wide circle of acquaintances and associations and an audience to receive as well as to criticize his creative efforts.

The urban university that does not aggressively seek for itself a role in fostering the arts is evading a task that it is peculiarly equipped to perform. Not only is support for the artist compatible with the purpose of a university, for if it is proper to study the theory and history of the arts it is also proper to engage in the practice of them. A university can also contribute to a stable institutional base for the arts not always to be found outside academic circles. August Heckscher, cultural adviser to President Kennedy, noted that we tend to underrate the institutional framework for the arts in this country. Our big task, he asserted, is to build institutions of the arts not only to support the artist but also to acquire "a sharp edge of excellence." He continued that "the educational sector is the liveliest segment of American culture, and that is good because Americans are more likely to accept the arts if they are education-sponsored rather than patron-sponsored which has snobbish connotations in our country."[9] The cultural life of such cities as Boston, Buffalo, Los Angeles, Louisville, Milwaukee, Minneapolis, New Haven, Pittsburgh, and Rochester has been considerably enhanced because universities in those cities have moved into the performing arts and have accepted increasing responsibility for training the professional artist.

Yet a great deal of the cultural activity in our metropolitan areas has taken place without evidence of university interest. Universities have not provided an adequate institutional base to support the performing artist. The problem of finding dignified employment for the artist has become aggravated in recent years, with proprietary and independent schools finding the struggle to exist difficult. Rising costs, accreditation, and competition with multipurpose institutions that offer, in addition to a professional curriculum, a broad general education have made it more hazardous for the independent school to survive.

Shortage of opportunity, financial insecurity, and reliance upon employment not connected with the arts are chronic problems facing the American artist. Countless first-rate artists are unable to find professional security and at the same time pursue their talents without jeopardizing their individuality. Actors' Equity, which regularly reports thousands seeking jobs on Broadway with only a few hundred to be placed, complained that "it is a sad anomaly of the wealthiest society the world has ever known that very few artists, however capable or hard working, are able to make a living by the practice of the fine arts alone." In a similar vein, former Secretary of Labor Goldberg, in a statement accompanying the findings in the Metropolitan Opera dispute, concluded that "America has a long way to go before our musicians, performers, and creative artists are accorded the dignity and honor to which their contribution to American life entitles them."[10] Of the 1,401 symphonies in the United States, only 54, or 4 per cent have 80 per cent or more of their performers who are professional musicians. And for the vast majority of these, full-time employment is not available, with the average salary ranging from $2,000 to $9,000.[11] These musicians must, therefore, find outside employment, in music or some other field. The plight of the professional dancer is even more critical, with only two or three of our large metropolitan centers able to support companies with any degree of stability.

Yet there are ways in which the university located in the city can contribute to the stability and security of the professional artist. Professional musicians can perform a dual role of teaching in the university and finding a place in the established cultural organizations of the community. Minneapolis and Louisville are examples of useful relationships that can develop between town and gown. For the creative artist, the opportunity to display in the city to a wide audience differing from the university community, and to expose his work to wide review, is also of great importance to his professional growth. The practice, which has now gained considerable support on many campuses, of the appointment of artists in residence—creative writers, musicians, painters, playwrights— is a further step in giving the artist security as well as professional status. Such persons permanently in residence on campus, and with something important to say or portray, can contribute to the development of high standards of taste and appreciation among students who might otherwise not be exposed to such experiences.

Chamber music is an especially suitable activity for a university to undertake. While there is growing interest in this field, it has not yet found a stable institutional base. By its very nature, it requires the intimacy of a small hall. Its box office potential, therefore, is limited, while costs are comparatively high. University sponsorship can contribute to its stability and acceptance. Such notable groups as the Fine Arts Quartet and the Budapest String Quartet have now found residence on urban university campuses and are serving not only as performing musicians but as master teachers as well. In this way chamber music is being elevated to an important place in the musical life of the university and the community.

In the city plays and music are performed, and art exhibits abound. Every sort of group meets to discuss science, art, religion, the humanities, and life itself. Cities are places where people congregate and where culture is free to grow and flourish. But too often the urban university student is not prepared for the city's assets. In the home he has not been exposed to cultural pursuits. His need to work while attending the university has often deprived him of leisure time needed to broaden his interests. The urban university student, inclined to be parochial in his outlook and often coming from a limited background, can benefit substantially by contact with people who are at home in the arts.

The urban university should therefore take the initiative in systematically presenting the best that the city has to offer and in supplementing these offerings with its own cultural and artistic fare. Faced with the question of what could be done during the lunch hour, the University of Wisconsin-Milwaukee scheduled a series of free noonday concerts by the Fine Arts Quartet, now in residence at that institution. An overflow audience which sat in the aisles and crouched on the stage, while others were turned away for lack of room, was enthralled by a performance of Haydn's "Quartet in D-minor, Op. 76, No. 2," and Prokofiev's "Quartet No. 1, Op. 50," with commentary interspersed during the program by members of the quartet. Few students at the university could have paid the prevailing price to hear a similar performance downtown. Yet a means was found to expose them to quality music, with such enthusiastic response that regular programing of this sort is now available at noontime without cost. A coordinated cultural program, which combines the rich offerings to be found in every major city with the substantial resources of the university, can assist the urban student in attaining a high level of appreciation in the broad areas of culture.

The urban university is markedly different from its nonurban counterpart in that it is but one of many cultural institutions in the community interested in promoting the arts. The larger the city, the greater the variety of cultural activities, and for this reason the more essential the need for the university to define its special place. In smaller communities, by way of contrast, the college often is the primary force in making available a wide variety of cultural experiences to the public. It brings to its community cultural events that would otherwise pass it by. It thereby fills a culture vacuum, making an important contribution to the enrichment of life in the community. So important has this activity become that "a new class of campus culture managers" has emerged, who generate audiences for the arts not only on the college campus but in the community as well.[12]

The urban university has quite a different opportunity by virtue of its setting. This is not to say that it does not have a role to play in bringing artists of renown to the campus. But this should not be its primary responsibility. Often the urban university overplays its impresario role and does not coordinate its cultural activities with those of the city, or present the unusual and innovational. The urban university that presents only the traditional cultural activities loses a significant opportunity to support esoteric activities that are representative of the cutting edge of the cultural frontier. For in a society where culture has become a status symbol, accepted by the great mass of people, with many superficial manifestations and a careless mouthing of artistic jargon, it is important for the university to lengthen the range of man's aesthetic and intellectual experience and provide an opportunity to meet head on a provocative idea, a play, a piece of literature, or a painting.

With the broad exposure that the arts are now receiving, it is important that an institution such as the university exists, where the high standards of the performing artist can be nurtured, where he can preserve his integrity and have full opportunity to fulfill his creative role in society. August Heckscher suggested that the

disinterested and considerate help of the artist is particularly necessary because of the mass nature of our society. The innovator too far in advance of his times or too independent of current trends and fashions is likely to find the great audience unwilling to listen. The performer who does get the ear of his audience, moreover, is subject to subtle temptations and pressures to compromise the quality of his work. The existence of the popular arts in their present pervasive and insatiable forms provides, indeed, one of the obstacles to the highest development of the fine arts. The need is to make possible fruitful interaction between the artist and the mass audience, but at the same time to give the artist the means of keeping a life somewhat apart, under conditions allowing him to develop in his own way and at his own pace.[13]

With increased costs and inadequate financial support continuing to plague the arts, there is in every community a tendency to compromise, to seek the lowest common denominator, to concentrate on the familiar. Few entrepreneurs are willing to risk the uncertain and the untried. As the arts are brought closer to the people, the university must set standards and support excellence, for quality and mass exposure are not incompatible as long as a clear distinction between the two is maintained. World premieres, avant-garde performances, new repertory, concert debuts, and unusual and seldom performed works are especially suitable for university audiences. Here experimentation and the new are received with greater enthusiasm than in the more conventional setting of the community.

Recognizing this unique role, the School of Fine Arts at the University of Wisconsin-Milwaukee has deliberately set out to be innovative in its academic offerings and in its general cultural programing. Its curriculum is based on the interrelationship of all the arts, with every student required to take two-year core courses— the Arts and Mankind, a survey of the various arts and their historical relationships, and Theory and Criticism, in which works in theater, music, art, dance, and literature are evaluated. On the programing side it has presented the first Beethoven Festival in the country, encompassing all the major forms used by the composer—orchestral, chamber, choral, and piano music; a summer arts festival with as many as 15 visiting artists on campus to teach and perform; noonday concerts of high quality; a number of American premieres such as Pinter's *The Dumb Waiter* and Rene-Jean Clot's *The Revelation*, and such first American performances as Bach's "Sinfonia Concertante in C Major" for flute, oboe, violin, violoncello, and orchestra.

Universities have a unique opportunity to help create a climate in which the arts can flourish. The development of the arts should not be limited to a few large cultural centers such as the Lincoln Center in New York City or the National Cultural Center in Washington, for one of the characteristics of the cultural explosion in this country has been its wide geographic diffusion. The Rockefeller Panel reported on the dramatic expansion of the arts in this country in the past two decades—a doubling in the number of symphony orchestras and groups presenting opera, an increase of

15 per cent in the number of theatrical enterprises, and a doubling of the amount of money paid for admissions to the performing arts, now running well over $400 million a year.[14] This interest in the arts, however,

will probably not by itself be enough to affect seriously the artistic life of the country. It is by its very nature diffuse, often shallow, frequently whimsical. Thus, the thrust in all activities organized on behalf of the arts is to stabilize the interest and to underpin it by providing, along with exposure to the arts, the understanding and the standards to measure them by.[15]

At a time, then, when decentralization of the arts is taking place in America and the arts are being brought close to the people, with all of the dangers inherent in mass exposure to the arts, the urban university has an unparalleled opportunity to contribute quality and excellence. By assuming the role of standard setter and friendly critic it can assist in creating a better climate for the arts. Not only is this a proper extension of the traditional role of the university; it is a necessary one, if the arts are to flourish.

CHAPTER VII

The City and the University:
Challenge and Response

URBANISM HAS BECOME THE DOMINANT ELEMENT IN OUR CUL-
ture, and in the years ahead more people will be conditioned by
an urban society that is in a continuous state of flux. If the urban
university is to fulfill its mission and improve the quality of urban
life, its resources must be organized so that the accumulated knowledge of the past as well as current findings can be put to work.
Because the scope of its activities is vast and far-reaching, it can
immeasurably improve society.

What follows, then, are the challenges to an urban university of
an urban culture and the responses necessary for coping with them
successfully.

CHALLENGES	RESPONSES
Many of the problems of our metropolitan areas are already well ahead of our best efforts to deal with them, with the present disarray of the urban scene ag-	Since universities provide leadership for the betterment of our society, they must now work to improve urban life, using an effort comparable in depth and breadth

CHALLENGES

gravated by the increasing complexities of city life.

Problems related to social and economic strain, racial tension, religious conflict, and nationality differences have become more severe and demand sympathetic and systematic treatment.

The fiscal crisis, the structure of local government, the economic interdependence of our metropolitan areas, the process of urban dispersal, the impoverished and disadvantaged, are basic problems facing every major city.

Innovation and experimentation have been conspicuously absent in most metropolitan communities of America. This is a role which the politician and the civic leader are often reluctant to assume.

More fact finding is needed as a prerequisite not only to urban policy making, but also to a general upgrading of all levels of performance in the urban field.

The recruitment and training of tomorrow's manpower has already reached acute proportions. The

RESPONSES

to that undertaken during the past century to enrich life on field and farm.

No community issue should be beyond the interest of the urban university. A university by definition has the obligation to preserve, discover, and transmit the whole of knowledge, and must work to understand and discern the problems of the metropolitan area.

Not being circumscribed by the geographic limits of a single community, the urban university can contribute to the development of urban theory and policy that is general in scope and universal in application.

Universities are uniquely equipped, through research and experimentation, to provide fresh ideas that can help meet the requirements of an urban society.

Investigation and experimentation, confirmation of fact, testing, refinement and evaluation, are peculiarly suitable to the university scholar and can be effectively applied to the urban scene.

Universities have traditionally trained personnel to meet the needs of society. Urban universities

CHALLENGES

RESPONSES

need for well trained personnel who have a general comprehension of urban problems is becoming more critical every year.

should now extend this tradition to the field of urban affairs.

The need for urban specialists is constantly expanding within the private as well as the public sector. At the same time state, regional, and federal governments are competing with local governments for a variety of urban specialists.

All the major disciplines of the university should be called upon to provide trained professional manpower for our cities: in commerce, engineering, education, architecture, the arts and the sciences, medicine and health, and social welfare.

The urban dweller needs a wide variety of services to help him adjust to the urban environment and to improve the quality of urban life. The problems he faces are complex and do not lend themselves to simple solutions.

The university should do for the urbanite what the land-grant colleges have done for the nation's farm population, taking the knowledge of the scholar into the community and extending the outreach of its influence to all phases of urban life. The university can undertake projects that have more than local significance and that can contribute some scientific validity to urban problems everywhere.

Urban life makes alien demands upon people who have been brought up in a nonurban culture. Family life, interpersonal relationships, community pressures, patterns of work and play—all present to the city dweller new and constantly changing challenges.

Neither the complexity nor the controversial nature of many of our urban problems should deter universities from developing new techniques and approaches. Creative innovation, rather than the performance of routine urban services, is the special role of the university in urban extension.

The acute needs of the disadvantaged of our cities, while they defy

New criteria and techniques must be developed if the urban uni-

CHALLENGES

simple description, have begun to reach crisis proportions.

Blight, obsolescence, and a steady environmental decline have occurred in many neighborhoods surrounding urban universities.

High land costs, circumscribed acreage, limited opportunities for expansion, and neighborhood apprehension about the university's intentions are all urgent concerns.

The neighborhood surrounding the urban university often comprises an institutional district, with many cultural, educational, and charitable institutions in close proximity to each other. Frequently the university serves as a magnet to draw other institutions, which find common cause with it and need to seek solutions to common problems.

RESPONSES

versity is to reach the disadvantaged of our cities.

The urban university must assist in reversing the tide of urban decline, and actively participate in redevelopment, rehabilitation, and conservation programs. Many advantages exist if its neighborhood has stability and a healthy environment.

Urban universities must think in terms of a new urban form, relevant to the metropolitan setting. The advantages of high rise construction, the use of subterranean space, intensive land use, the building of facilities within easy walking distance of each other, and the use of intervening spaces between buildings for plazas and gathering places to facilitate human interaction are factors that should be utilized in planning an urban campus.

The urban university must relate itself intimately to all of the institutions in the area as well as the neighborhood in which it is located. The university should make both its long and short range intentions known in an informative and understandable manner.

CHALLENGES	RESPONSES
The university often makes demands on the city for additional services, takes property off the tax rolls as it expands, and disrupts the normal life of the neighborhood in which it is located.	The urban university brings many tangible benefits to the city. In addition to its cultural advantages, it is often a large employer and purchaser, contributes substantially to building and construction, attracts countless visitors to the city, and is a major factor in the establishment of nearby industrial and research parks.
An increasingly large number of college students will be coming from lower income families. With costs continuing to rise, the availability of a college education at home will become more urgent.	Universities located in cities can give many who would otherwise be denied a college education a chance to continue their education with a minimum of financial outlay, but a maximum of opportunity.
A large untapped reservoir of high ability among our youth is now lost. This is notably true among the culturally and economically disadvantaged of our cities where a vast supply of undeveloped talent exists.	The urban university can provide an outlet for the educational ambitions of these able youths and help bring into reality the promise of democracy that everyone, regardless of race, religion, or economic and social status, should be educated to the limits of his ability.
The big city provides singular opportunities for diversified employment for the student.	Since these opportunities provide the means not only to finance a student's education, but also to contribute to the maintenance and support of the family, the urban university should assist in every way possible in developing coordinated programs of financial aid and employment for the student.

CHALLENGES

The city's courts, hospitals and clinics, churches, schools, industries, mass media, social centers, and welfare agencies provide an educational laboratory without parallel.

RESPONSES

Cooperative programs with industry, work-study arrangements with community agencies, internships, as well as other off-campus operations, offer great promise to the student if properly developed and coordinated by the urban university.

The explosion of knowledge, the impact of automation, and increased leisure make the demand for continuing education greater than ever.

The urban university needs to develop programs especially designed for adults gainfully employed, as well as for others who are seeking further avenues for self-fulfillment and enjoyment.

Every major city in the United States has untold cultural resources that enrich life and that distinguish it from smaller communities. These are what give vitality and spirit to the city.

The university located in the city should fully utilize these rich cultural resources. They can be of inestimable value to the artist in residence, to the faculty members who are specializing in one of the arts or who find enjoyment in them, and to the urban student who often has not been fully exposed to all that the city has to offer.

Cultural activities are increasingly important in the lives of our people.

Since the encouragement of the arts is in keeping with the broad purposes of both the university and society, training in the creative arts should now be added to theory, interpretation, history, and criticism as a proper university function.

With the broad support that the arts are now receiving, and with

The university located in the city can create a better climate in which

CHALLENGES	RESPONSES
more people participating in amateur art, this mass exposure provides a broad base of interest, but tends to concentrate on the familiar and the popular. Nor does it always insure excellence.	the arts can flourish by engaging in innovation and experimentation.

Our society is irretrievably urban. Since our cities are here to stay, the time is at hand to take a new look at them. It is urgent that a major effort be made to reshape them. This will require serious reflection, and positive action. In all of these matters the urban university can play a central role. It can, in fact, become the single most important force in the re-creation of our cities.

There is no question that we have the means physically to rebuild our cities. Massive expressway construction, symbolized by the rampaging bulldozer, and dramatic physical transformation leave no doubt that the face of our cities is rapidly being changed. We are certain to make headway in solving some of our most pressing urban problems. Traffic congestion and air and water pollution will reach such proportions that people will have no choice but to act. Housing, urban renewal, and the revitalizing of our central cities, too, are manageable goals.

But the aims and ends of city life are not so readily attained. One of our greatest needs is to raise the level of comprehension about the purposes and goals of urban civilization above that of mere living to one of enjoyment, pleasure, and fulfillment. How little we really know and have done about the character of our cities, compared with advances in science and technology. Existing knowledge, research, training, and practice still fall short of giving us guidelines for the rebuilding of our cities. Yet it is in the areas of investigation and fact finding, and of applying the knowledge of the scholar to the practical problems of city life, that urban universities can make their most distinctive contribution.

Modern cities too often have been influenced more by the pressures of technology and industrialization than by any overriding concern for the needs of the community and of man as a part of it. Thus in our current efforts to rebuild, the needs of human beings to live and realize their potential have not been taken into full account. Over 2,000 years ago Aristotle wrote that the city exists "for the sake of the good life." Yet today our cities are, in fact, contributing to the dehumanization of our people. Fundamental changes in both outlook and policy are needed if our cities are to nurture "the good life" which not only serves man's material needs, but also satisfies his spirit and soul. Since our universities possess the broadly based knowledge of many disciplines, have as their purpose the creation of an intellectual climate necessary to achieve objectivity and perspective, and have experience in relating learning to the needs of society, they are equipped to perform a task that no other institution can do as well. Here, then, is a unique role for our urban universities—that of giving meaning to urban life and assisting in the creation of a new image for our cities.

Notes

I. A Profile of the Urban University

1. For fuller treatment see Lowrie S. Daly, S.J., *The Medieval University*, New York, 1961, chap. 6, pp. 193-195.

2. Kermit Parsons, "A Truce in the War Between Universities and Cities," *The Journal of Higher Education*, January 1963, p. 18.

3. *Ibid.*, p. 17.

4. Frederick Rudolph, *The American College and University*, New York, 1962, pp. 87-88.

5. S. P. Capen, "Program for Progress in Education," *The Educational Record*, January 1923, pp. 6-7.

6. T. R. McConnell, *A General Pattern for American Public Higher Education*, New York, 1962, pp. 2-3.

7. Edward Power, *A History of Catholic Higher Education in the United States*, Milwaukee, 1958, p. 172.

8. Charles W. Eliot, "The New Education. Its Organization," *Atlantic Monthly*, March 1869, p. 364.

9. For a detailed analysis refer to an address by John Rettaliata, president, Illinois Institute of Technology, reported in *Summary of Proceedings, 47th Annual Meeting of the Association of Urban Universities*, 1961, pp. 58-64.

10. John Rettaliata, "Special Resources for Scientific and Technological Education in an Urban Environment," *Summary of Proceedings, 47th*

Annual Meeting of the Association of Urban Universities, 1961, p. 58.

11. R. H. Eckelberry, "The History of the Municipal University in the United States," *Office of Education Bulletin No. 2*, 1932, p. 173.

12. *Ibid.*, pp. 169–170.

13. William Carlson, *The Municipal University*, Washington, D.C., 1962, p. 99.

14. Christian K. Arnold, "Community Campuses of State Universities," *Saturday Review*, March 17, 1962, p. 92.

15. Carlson, p. 7.

16. *Summary of Proceedings, 15th Annual Meeting of the Association of Urban Universities*, 1928, p. 9.

17. *Summary of Proceedings, 42nd Annual Meeting of Association of Urban Universities*, 1956, pp. 14–15.

18. *Summary of Proceedings, 46th Annual Meeting of the Association of Urban Universities*, 1960, p. 17.

19. John S. Diekhoff, *Democracy's College*, New York, 1950, p. 30.

20. Donald R. McNeil, "Crisis in University Adult Education," *NUEA Spectator*, Vol. XXVIII, No. 3, February–March 1963.

21. Henry Steele Commager, "Is Ivy Necessary?", *Saturday Review*, September 17, 1960, p. 88.

22. Sidney Tickton, "A Third Force in College Enrollments," *Saturday Review*, March 21, 1964, pp. 70–71.

23. Henry Heald, "The Universities' Role in Reshaping American Cities," paper read at conference on The Role of the University in an Urban Setting, Milwaukee, Wisconsin, October 28–29, 1960.

II. The University and the Urban Scene

1. Henry Steele Commager, "Is Ivy Necessary?", *Saturday Review*, September 17, 1960, p. 89.

2. Adna Ferrin Weber, *The Growth of Cities in the Nineteenth Century*, Ithaca, New York, 1963, p. 21.

3. Orin F. Nolting and David S. Arnold, eds., *The Municipal Year Book, 1962*, Chicago, 1962, p. 31.

4. J. P. Pickard, ed., *Metropolitanization of the U.S.*, published by Urban Land Institute of Washington, D.C., 1959, p. 8.

5. Harrison E. Salisbury, book review, *The New York Times*, October 5, 1958, Section VII, p. 1.

6. Luther Gulick, "Five Challenges in Today's New Urban World," *American City*, December 1956, pp. 149–150.

7. Robert Wood, "Urban Prospects: 1970 and Beyond," *The Wisconsin Academy Looks at Urbanism*, May 1963, pp. 20–21.

8. Fred Harvey Harrington, "The Function of University Administration," *The Journal of Higher Education*, March 1963, pp. 131–132.

9. Eric Walker, "Reorganization for Progress," *Phi Kappa Phi Journal*, Spring 1961, p. 28.

10. For fuller treatment of this subject see Morton and Lucia White, *The Intellectual Versus the City*, Harvard University Press and the MIT Press, 1962.

11. Robert Walker, "The Poet and the Rise of the City," *Mississippi Valley Historical Review*, June 1962, XLIX, 98–99.

12. *Pittsburgh Post Gazette*, November 6, 1963.

13. Wood, pp. 12–13.

14. Edward Eddy, *Colleges for our Land and Time*, New York, 1957, pp. 72–73.

15. For detailed treatment of this subject see address by Paul Ylvisaker, *Summary of Proceedings, 44th Annual Meeting of the Association of Urban Universities*, 1958, pp. 46-55.

16. Michael Oakeshott, "The Universities," *Cambridge Journal, II,* 1949, p. 523.

17. *Preliminary Report* to special Regent Committee on the future of the University of Wisconsin-Milwaukee, February 4, 1963.

18. John Gardner, "Preserving Quality in Higher Education," *Summary of Proceedings, 43rd Annual Meeting of the Association of Urban Universities*, 1957, pp. 16-17.

19. For an enlargement of this point of view see James Coke, "Ways and Means for Urban Universities to Exercise a Unique Function in their Communities," *University and Community*, Proceedings of Wingspread Conference, April 25–26, 1963, Racine, Wisconsin, p. 15.

20. For fuller treatment of this subject see W. A. Robson, *Great Cities of the World*, New York, 1954, Part I.

21. *School and Society*, IV, 1916, p. 86.

22. Joseph Hudnut, *Architecture and the Spirit of Man*, Harvard University Press, 1949, p. 262.

III. Urban Needs and University Resources

1. Orin F. Nolting and David S. Arnold, eds., *The Municipal Year Book 1963*, Chicago, 1963, p. 7.
2. Municipal Manpower Commission, *Governmental Manpower for Tomorrow's Cities*, New York, 1962.
3. *The Municipal Year Book 1962*, p. 190.
4. *Governmental Manpower for Tomorrow's Cities*, pp. 20–21.
5. *The Municipal Year Book 1963*, p. 1.
6. *The Municipal Year Book 1963*, p. 22.
7. *The Municipal Year Book 1963*, p. 46.
8. Harvey Perloff, *Education for Planning*, Baltimore, 1957, pp. 4–5.
9. *Ibid.*, p. 11.
10. David Popenoe, "The University in Training for the Urban Age," *University and Community*, Proceedings of Wingspread Conference, April 25–26, 1963, Racine, Wisconsin, p. 104.
11. Perloff, pp. 104–105.
12. *The Rockefeller Panel Reports*, "The Pursuit of Excellence: Education and the Future of America," p. 350.
13. *Governmental Manpower for Tomorrow's Cities*, p. 24.
14. *The Rockefeller Panel Reports*, p. 350.
15. Harlan Cleveland, "Education for Public Complexity," *Public Management*, December 1959, p. 283.
16. *Third Progress Report to the Ford Foundation*, The University, Madison, Wisconsin, August 19, 1963, pp. 4–5 (mimeographed).
17. *Governmental Manpower for Tomorrow's Cities*, p. 121.
18. Lewis Mumford, *The City in History*, New York, 1961.
19. For a full description see *The Dartmouth Story: Undergraduate Education for Urban Life and Urban Affairs*, by H. Wentworth Eldredge and Atlee E. Shidler, published by the Washington Center for Metropolitan Studies, 1962.
20. Robert Wood, "The Contributions of Political Science to Urban Form," in *Urban Life and Form*, edited by Werner Hirsch, 1963, pp. 122–123.
21. P. W. Bridgman, "The Prospect for Intelligence," *Yale Review*, Spring 1945, p. 450.
22. Coleman Woodbury, "Bringing the Resources of the University

to the Community Through Research," paper read at conference on The Role of the University in an Urban Setting, Milwaukee, Wisconsin, October 28–29, 1960.

23. "The Talk of the Town," *New Yorker*, January 17, 1948, p. 17.

24. Peter Rossi and Robert Dentler, *The Politics of Urban Renewal*, New York, 1961, pp. 33–37.

25. Scott Greer, "Ways and Means for Urban Universities to Exercise a Unique Function in their Communities," Proceedings of Wingspread Conference, April 25–26, 1963, p. 19.

26. Daniel Wilner *et al.*, *The Housing Environment and Family Life*, The Johns Hopkins Press, 1962.

27. Ben West, "The Challenge of the City to the Urban University," paper read at conference on The Role of the University in an Urban Setting, Milwaukee, Wisconsin, October 28–29, 1960.

28. Robert Gutman, "Urban Studies as a Field of Research," *The American Behavioral Scientist*, February 1963, pp. 12–13.

29. Merle Curti, "A New Golden Age for Social Studies at Wisconsin," unpublished address at dedication of University of Wisconsin Center, April 11, 1958.

30. Charles McCarthy, *The Wisconsin Idea*, New York, 1912, pp. 137–139.

31. University of Wisconsin Urban Program pamphlet entitled *New Frontiers in University Service to the State of Wisconsin*, p. 9.

32. *New York Times*, June 21, 1964, p. 39.

33. *Summary of Proceedings, 44th Annual Meeting of the Association of Urban Universities*, 1958, p. 54.

34. *Third Progress Report to the Ford Foundation*, The University of Madison, Wisconsin, August 19, 1963, pp. 42–43 (mimeographed).

35. John Bebout, "University Services to the Urban Community," *The American Behavioral Scientist*, February 1963, p. 45.

36. Abraham Flexner, *Universities—American, English, German*, New York, 1930, pp. 5–6.

37. For a fuller treatment of this matter see Kirk Petshek, "A New Role for City Universities—Urban Extension Programs," in *Journal of the American Institute of Planners*, November 1964, pp. 304–316.

38. For a more detailed description of this program see Paul Goodman, "Columbia's Unorthodox Seminars," *Harper's Magazine*, January 1964, pp. 72–82.

39. Bebout, p. 31.

40. *Congressional Record*, January 12, 1965.

IV. THE URBAN CAMPUS

1. Glenn Dumke, "Moving San Francisco State College to a New Site," in *Case Book on Campus Planning and Institutional Development*, 1962, United States Government Printing Office, Washington, D. C., pp. 72–92.

2. *New Campuses for Old: A Case Study of Four Colleges that Moved*, 1962, Educational Facilities Laboratories, N. Y.

3. Millard Gladfelter, *Association of Urban Universities Newsletter*, XV, No. 4, May–June 1963, p. 3.

4. Fred Hechinger, "Campus vs. Slums," *The New York Times*, October 1, 1961, Section E, p. 7.

5. B. T. Fitzpatrick, *Assistance for Colleges and Universities Located In or Near Urban Renewal Areas*, American Council on Education; Committee on Urban Renewal, September 1961, pp. 2–3.

6. *L'expansion de la Recherche Scientifique*, Numero 7, November 1960, pp. 27–31.

7. *Times Educational Supplement*, London, June 14, 1963, p. 1306.

8. For a condensed summarization of the report see the *Times Educational Supplement*, London, October 25, 1963.

9. Harry Ree, "Seven in the Sixties," *Saturday Review*, August 17, 1963, p. 36.

10. Julian Levi, "The Influence of Environment on Urban Institutions," *Educational Record*, April 1961, p. 137.

11. Henry Commager, "Is Ivy Necessary?", *Saturday Review*, September 17, 1960, p. 70.

12. Julian Levi, "Expanding the University of Chicago," in *Case Book on Campus Planning and Institutional Development*, 1962, U.S. Government Printing Office, Washington, D.C., p. 109.

13. *New York Times*, January 13, 1965, p. 95.

14. The story is told by Julian Levi in the article referred to in Note 12, above.

15. Levi, p. 126.

16. *New York Times*, January 13, 1965, p. 95.

17. *Wall Street Journal*, April 15, 1963, p. 1.

18. *Parking Programs for Universities*, University Facilities Research Center, Madison, Wisconsin, November 1961, pp. 13–14.

19. David B. Carlson, "Town and Gown," *Architectural Forum*, March 1963, p. 93.

20. Neil Carothers, "University Circle Institutions Round Out Urban Site," in *College and University Business*, May 1963, p. 57.

21. *Statement of Problems and Goals for the General Neighborhood Renewal Plan*, Morningside-Columbia University, pp. 1–3.

22. Catherine J. Tilson, *Yale in New Haven*, New Haven, 1962, pp. 11–12.

23. *Ibid.*, pp. 8–9.

24. Reginald C. McGrane, *The University of Cincinnati: A Success Story in Urban Higher Education*, New York, 1963, pp. 344–345.

25. Edward Litchfield, *The University and the Economy*, January 29, 1963, Pittsburgh, pp. 5–6.

26. John Fischer, "Money Bait," *Harper's Magazine*, September 1961, p. 12.

27. Adams, Howard & Greeley; Anderson, Beckwith & Haible, City Planning Consultants, *University Circle, A Plan for Its Development*, August 1957, Cleveland, Ohio, p. 51.

V. The Urban University Student

1. David Henry, "Crisis for State Universities," in *U.S. News and World Report*, February 1, 1965, p. 58.

2. "College Going in Wisconsin's Seventy-One Counties," prepared by Joint Staff of the Coordinating Committee of Higher Education, December 1961.

3. J. Kenneth Little, "Trends Affecting Contemporary Educational Planning," *Journal of Higher Education*, April 1961, p. 195.

4. Thomas Evans Coulton, *A City College in Action*, New York, 1955, p. 7.

5. Henry Steele Commager, "Is Ivy Necessary?" *Saturday Review*, September 17, 1960, p. 86.

6. Jeannette H. Eilenberg, *Brooklyn College: Class Portrait 1953–1957*, p. 13.

7. For a somewhat different view of this matter see article by John

Kysar, "Mental Health in an Urban Commuter University," in *Archives of General Psychiatry*, November 1964, pp. 472–483.

8. *Social Forces Influencing American Education*, 60th Year Book of the National Society for the Study of Education, 1961, pp. 122–123.

9. *Ibid.*, p. 124.

10. Ordway Tead, *Summary of Proceedings of 32nd Annual Meeting of the Association of Urban Universities*, 1946, p. 101.

11. David Boroff, "The Case for the Asphalt Campus," *The New York Times Magazine*, April 21, 1963.

12. John S. Diekhoff, *Democracy's College*, New York, 1950, p. 28.

13. Frederick Rudolph, *The American College and University*, New York, 1962, p. 92.

14. John Friedmann, "Cities in Social Transformation," *Comparative Studies in Society and History*, IV, No. 1, November 1961, p. 88.

15. Reginald C. McGrane, *The University of Cincinnati: A Success Story in Urban Higher Education*, New York, 1963, p. 211.

16. *Cooperative Education Newsletter*, January 1965, p. 1.

17. See report on cooperative education: Ralph Tyler and Annicel Mius, *Summary of the National Study*, 1961, Thomas Alva Edison Foundation.

18. James W. Wilson and Edward H. Lyons, *Work-Study College Programs*, New York, 1961, pp. 155–158.

19. John Henry Cardinal Newman, *The Idea of a University*, London, 1852, p. 146.

20. Harold Case, *The Bulletin of the Association of College Unions*, October 1963, p. 8.

21. Commager, p. 70.

22. Robert Havighurst, *American Higher Education in the 1960's*, Columbus, Ohio, 1960, p. 33.

23. J. Kenneth Little, *Explorations into College Plans and Experiences of High School Graduates*, Madison, Wisconsin, 1959, p. 97.

24. *Expanding Opportunities: The Negro and Higher Education*, American Council on Education, II, No. 3, p. 2.

25. Havighurst, p. 70.

26. *The Federal Work-Study Concept: An Analysis*, June 1963, p. 11.

27. *Expanding Opportunities: The Negro and Higher Education*, American Council on Education, I, No. 1, p. 5.

28. The Rockefeller Panel Report, *Prospect for America*, Garden City, New York, 1961, p. 381.

29. Richard L. Plaut, *Blueprints for Talent Searching*, New York, 1957, pp. 32–34.

30. *The President's Committee on Education Beyond the High School*, July 1957, p. 8.

31. For a full treatment on this matter, see Dennis L. Trueblood, "The Role of the Counselor in the Guidance of Negro Students," *Harvard Educational Review*, Summer 1960.

32. Eli Ginzberg, *The Negro Potential*, New York, 1956, pp. 93–94.

33. For a fuller treatment, see *Expanding Opportunities: The Negro and Higher Education*, American Council on Education, II, Nos. 2 and 3.

34. Rockefeller Panel, p. 350, pp. 337–338.

VI. THE URBAN UNIVERSITY AND THE ARTS

1. Alexis de Tocqueville, *Democracy in America*, New York, 1840, pp. 35, 71, 72.

2. Arnold Mitchell, managing editor Long Range Planning Service, Stanford Research Institute, Menlo Park, California (unpublished speech), p. 8.

3. James Perkins, "The Universities and the Arts," Cornell University Centennial Celebration, March 9, 1965, p. 3.

4. *The Performing Arts: Problems and Prospects*, Rockefeller Panel Report, 1965, p. 182.

5. W. McNeil Lowry, "The University and the Creative Arts," *Arts in Society*, II, No. 3, p. 10.

6. The Harvard report in a slightly expanded form is to be found in *Arts in Society*, II, No. 3, under the heading "The Artist in the University" by George Wald, p. 58.

7. W. McNeil Lowry, vice-president of the Ford Foundation, examined this matter in an address given before the Association of Graduate Schools, October 24, 1961. This appears in *The Art Journal*, Summer 1962, p. 233; *Educational Theater Journal*, 1962 Supplement, p. 99, and *Arts in Society*, II, No. 3, p. 7.

8. John Ely Burchard, "The Limits of Utilitarianism," in *Metropolis:*

Values in Conflict, Wadsworth Publishing Co., Belmont, California, 1964, pp. 56–57.

9. From an article on August Heckscher by Frederick M. Winship in the *Milwaukee Journal*, November 16, 1962, part 1, p. 22.

10. Freda Goldman, "Resources on Behalf of the Arts in America," in *Arts in Society*, II, No. 2, pp. 108–109.

11. *The Performing Arts: Problems and Prospects*, Rockefeller Panel Report, p. 22.

12. For a more detailed treatment of this subject, see Alvin Toffler, *The Culture Consumers*, St. Martin's Press, New York, 1964, chap. 6.

13. August Heckscher, "The Quality of American Culture," in *Goals for Americans*, Columbia University, 1960, p. 134.

14. Rockefeller Panel Report, pp. 13–14.

15. Goldman, p. 109.

INDEX